Why You Should
Take Your
Travel Agent
to Lunch

Why You Should
Take Your
Travel Agent
to Lunch

101 Timely Tips For Travelers

HARRY KNITTER

WITH L. WILLIAM CHILES

Kordene Publications, Ltd.
Okemos, Michigan

Published by Kordene Publications, Ltd.
4463 Copperhill, Okemos, Michigan 48864

Publisher's Cataloging-in-Publication Data
Knitter, Harry W.
    Why you should take your travel agent to lunch: 101 timely tips
    for travelers / Harry Knitter — Okemos, Michigan :
    Kordene Publications, Ltd. c1997.
        p.   ill.   cm.
    Includes index.
    ISBN 0-9652333-1-6
    1. General Travel. 2. Business Travel.   3. Humor. I. Title.
GN365.9.J46   1997
910.2   dc—20   96-79656

PROJECT COORDINATION BY JENKINS GROUP

00 99 98 ❖   5 4 3 2 1

Printed in the United States of America

To Nancy
My inspiration for everything
that's important to me

and

To Don
Whose support, caring
and friendship
will be sorely missed

CONTENTS

PREFACE

W e have a great deal in common—
you, the traveler, and I, the travel provider. We both want smooth trips, good-value fares, comfortable accommodations, and glitch-free travel.

The one key ingredient to accomplishing all of this is the travel agent who has, as a priority mission, your best interests and objectives in mind.

Playing a role similar to the investment counselor who helps you handle your money wisely and the real estate agent who helps you make sound property decisions, the travel agent can be indispensable in assisting you to make and carry out your travel plans. Whether you're traveling across the state or around the globe, on business or for pleasure, a good travel agent can help you plan that trip more easily and, usually, more cost efficiently.

Yes, there is every good reason to take your travel agent to lunch. (And sometimes to dinner, too.) But first, it is important to choose that agent carefully...more carefully than you would normally choose a dining companion, because that agent is not only your travel investment counselor, but also can become your friend, confidant, and advocate when it comes to business or leisure travel.

The travel business is an extremely complex industry that is governed by an intricate superstructure of relationships and affiliations, governed by complicated regulations, and yet deregulated to the extent that prices seek and find their own levels. Travel is highly competitive, influenced by many different factors in the marketplace.

It takes a knowledgeable professional to find a way around this complicated and often frustrating business. The qualified travel agent is that individual — not simply an issuer of tickets, but an experienced professional who is knowledgeable about every phase of travel.

Choosing the *right* travel agent is crucial because, obviously, not all travel agents are equal.

I'm pleased to collaborate with Harry Knitter on this important book, which provides a fair and objective picture of the travel business as it exists today. Improving our service to customers is a serious challenge — but this business, at the core, is a fun business, and Harry captures some of its humorous dimensions, reminding us not to take ourselves or our businesses seriously all the time, but certainly most of the time.

L. William Chiles
CEO, Hickory Travel Systems

ACKNOWLEDGMENTS

If you read my first book, you would know that I didn't take the acknowledgments very seriously. Since then, I've learned that those who were the target of my whimsy didn't show me much when it came to senses of humor. Nuts to them; let them get their own book next time.

The second lesson I learned is that nobody even reads the Acknowledgments except the typesetter, proofreader and those people who expect to be mentioned. If you're the exception, consider yourself in exclusive and disgustingly limited company.

Respecting your persistence in actually examining this section, though, I guess I better give you some acknowledgments to read. So here you are:

First, my supportive family — my sons Andy, David, and Scott, daughter-in-law Leslie and her parents, John and Harriett Marenas, and our two grandbabies, Kayla and Nicholas — deserves my most sincere thanks for their encouragement and perseverance in listening to my limitless inventory of book stories and updates on my progress. (As for the currect positioning of my commas and semicolons, credit my editor-son Scott, who adeptly smoothes out all the rough spots).

Second, my brother Jim Knitter and his wife, Alice, have earned prominent mention for their enthusiastic efforts to promote *Holding Pattern* on their trips west. Thanks for all you do, guys, and happy future travels.

Next, I am grateful to a large number of co-operative travel agents who were generous with their time and input. Especially notable were my collaborator, Bill Chiles, of Hickory Travel Systems, Inc.; Kevin Hamilton, Marina Hawkins, Tom Kinder, Kathie Drolett, Jane DeGrow, Tammy Scheuer, Kris Trudgen, Bob Sorum, Sandy Thelen, Connie Root, Karen Izzo, and others. I'd particularly like to single out Pam Mitchell of Spartan Travel, who turned up on a miserable snowy Michigan evening to share her knowledge and experience with us.

My thanks, also, to my business colleagues, Lou Brand, Jim Doll and Shari Ghoddousi, who conveyed their interesting travel stories to me, as did Dr. Kenneth Marton, my optometrist, and Jim and Barb Pryor, close friends and fellow road warriors. And I'm pleased to extend my appreciation to Brenda Copley, my Administrative Assistant and Martha Keeler, both of whom performed magnificently as chief sounding boards and test market subjects. I also owe a lot to the Jenkins Group's Jerry Jenkins, who played a part in the conception of this book; Alex Moore, who put it all together; and Glynis Steadman, of Griffith and Associates, who put Bill Chiles and this project together.

And I can't forget Professor Linda Peckham of Lansing Community College, who continues to provide both encouragement and expert counsel to me and countless other aspiring authors and publishers. Finally, gratitude to Andrew Toos for another collection of outstanding cartoons.

If you're still with me, thanks for being interested and curious enough to want to read my work. I'm thrilled you actually paid something to buy my book. . . and I hope you'll find at least one or two tips that will save you more than enough to cover your cost. (You did pay for this book, didn't you — little rascal?)

Thanks to everyone who helped me turn the unfathomable into reality. This is proof that if you think you can, you probably can.

INTRODUCTION

The once-glamorous, once-prosperous American travel agency is enduring significant changes. In this era of capped commissions, discount travel brokers, and electronic mail via Internet, the challenges to tradition are considerable. In the time that it takes you to browse through my 101 tips for travelers, some local independent agencies — perhaps a few that have effectively served your needs in the past — will have closed their doors for the final time. Still others are drastically altering the way they do business, recognizing that the survival struggle is underway.

The beginning of the end for the travel agency business? On the contrary, the best days for travel agents and their customers like you and me are just ahead. But fundamental changes in this industry will reshape it between now and the turn of the century.

The causes of escalating turmoil are many, and they will be identified in the pages to follow. Why should you care? If you're a traveler, the reforms evolving out of this period of transition will have significant impact on your future trips. As you look toward future excursions, a clear understanding of what is happening in the travel industry will make it possible for you to maximize the benefits of working with a travel agent in your trip planning and ensure that you get full value for your travel dollars.

At present, travel agents are the leading distributors of travel products and services. According to the American Society of Travel Agents, they book 80% of all air travel, 30% of all hotel reservations, and 95% of all cruise reservations.

Those of us who travel frequently are constantly adjusting to changes that we didn't have to deal with in the past. We're seeing ticketless travel in its infancy. Security is tighter at airports than ever before, requiring travelers to arrive up to two hours before flight time. Air travelers have to identify themselves at every turn. Since deregulation, more people have been filling more flights. And, waiting time is greater than ever, causing some airports to evolve into innovative entertainment and shopping venues, rather than the sterile and dull people-hangars most airport terminals were designed to be prior to the 1970's.

Like *Holding Pattern: Airport Waiting Made Easy*, my first book, this guide will be helpful to travelers of all ages and stages of experience. If it enables you to comprehend the role of the agent and how best to work with yours, my mission will be accomplished. My style is to provide meaningful information first, and then plenty of opportunities to smile. I hope to elicit at least a few laughs from you, and I hope they will emerge in the right places.

Finally, I will offer you ideas and encouragement to make travel an integral part of your life, no matter what stage your age says you're in. Don't wait until retirement days to consider traveling on a regular basis. Make the time in your hectic schedule to plan your travel time just as diligently as you plan your business and social engagements, for travel adds dimension to our existence.

While this book is focused on the business of travel, it's really about people gaining enhanced fulfillment and happiness out of life. With all of the challenges and disappointments that everyday living presents to us in this volatile era, travel can be the elixir that prevents those challenges from overwhelming us and our loved ones. And in these days of dysfunctional family relationships, traveling together can often create positive memories that will live on in the archives of our family's most pleasant experiences.

It's almost time to depart. Before we leave, why don't we do lunch? My treat.

PART I

The Appetizers

1.

What? No Frequent Flyer Miles?

Time present and time past
Are both perhaps present in time future,
And time future contained in time past.

— T.S. Eliot

✈ · · · · · · · · · · I think that most present day travelers would agree that travel just ain't what it used to be. With a casual farewell wave to my family in 1958, I departed from Milwaukee's Billy Mitchell Field on my way to represent the University of Wisconsin—Milwaukee at the Collegiate Press Convention in New York, my first airline trip ever.

I didn't speed to the gate on a moving sidewalk, didn't pick up a *USA Today* to read on the plane, didn't call my voicemail before boarding, and didn't get credited with frequent flyer miles for the trip. The reason? None of those accoutrements existed when I began my travel experiences.

Nor did I have access to:

◆ Jumbo jets
◆ Wheelie bags

- ◆ CNN Airport Network®
- ◆ Toll-free phone lines
- ◆ Sony Walkmans®
- ◆ The Concorde®
- ◆ Laptop computers
- ◆ Airport shops other than the newsstand
- ◆ Travel agents with computer access to the latest flight information
- ◆ Airphones®
- ◆ Ticketless travel
- ◆ Business facilities in the airport terminal
- ◆ Cellular phones
- ◆ Competitors to AT&T®
- ◆ Mileage credit cards

Yet, with all of these contemporary amenities, travel today is more of a hassle than it was then because there were fewer air travelers, we moved about freely without barriers like X-ray machines, and airports were generally much smaller and more compact. With fares regulated by the federal government, there were no fare wars nor resulting hordes of passengers on most flights.

Of course, there were downsides as well. For example, in some airports, it was necessary to dig out your own luggage from a wheeled cart outside of the terminal. And since there were no national toll-free numbers, we had to track down the local offices of airlines to make or revise flight reservations. Many of them were only available during limited hours each day.

One element that hasn't changed: questionable-quality airline food. Of course, it wasn't heated up in microwave ovens, but it was just as mediocre and full of fat calories as it is on most of the present day flights. But today you are served fewer meals . . . which, in the long run, is probably a good thing.

The chapters that follow represent the highlights of my travel experiences over the years, as well as a few choice recollections contributed by friends.   I hope you enjoy going along for the ride.

2.

You Can Do It Yourself–But Why?

The real meaning of travel, like that of a conversation by the fireside, is the discovery of oneself through contact with other people...

—Paul Tournier

Okay, I admit it. I sometimes act like an insidious control freak. I insist on taking my own dress shirts to the Korean laundry every Saturday morning to make sure they're meticulously prepared "on hangers, no starch," without variation. I also buy my own breakfast cereal, so that I get to enjoy a certain brand of crunchy granola with a touch of honey, and avoid that puffy wheaty stuff that's supposed to be better for me. And I occasionally try to make my own flight reservations directly with the airlines.

I call. I listen to the recorded message ("All our agents are busy, but your call is important to us. . .blah, blah, and blah") and I wait some more while the strains of elevator music from the 1960's put me into a trance. A robotic voice breaks in (recorded, of course), tells me that the calls will be answered in the order they were received, and informs me that my call is important. Then the robotic voice hangs up and they play a commercial extolling the virtues of the island of Lumbago (the commercial sounds great, but I can't respond because all lines are busy).

Finally, a real live person's monotone voice answers. And then the questions begin. Where am I planning to go? When? Alone? What time? How will I pay for the ticket? What's my VISA number? Expiration date? And on. And on.

I ask the dreaded "P" word question, "p-p-p-price." The voice commands me to wait just a moment. *Click.* I'm on "hold" again, listening to 1950's elevator music.

All this time, I'm thinking, "Why am I doing this? I've got work to do, books to be written, and I really don't need these unnerving delays. Isn't there a better way?"

Fortunately, there is. It's called The Travel Agent.

Making the same flight arrangements described above, but this time through a travel agent, I would have dialed a local number, talked to a friendly, familiar voice, told them what I wanted to do, where and when I wanted to travel, and hung up the phone.

Frequent flyer number? I can never find it when I want it, but I don't need it, 'cause the agent's computer has it memorized. The sneaky little machine and its mouse mate also know that I prefer to sit on an aisle, forward in the cabin, and need a special salt-free meal. When I arrive, I will prefer a mid-sized Chrysler rental car and a smoke-free room with a queen-sized bed on the lower floors of the hotel. Hot damn! The computer remembers those idiosyncratic "must-haves," too!

How will I know I got the best price? With computer access to all of the confusing major airline fare schedules, my agent — who wants my business for life — will do her absolute best to locate the most favorable fares on the date and at the time I want to fly.

Effective travel agents know how to maneuver discreetly with the airline and supplier representatives to ensure their customer — you — is satisfied. After all, they rely on repeat business to keep the doors open, so they work hard to make sure you're still smiling when you return from your journey. If you paid more than you should have, you're not likely to smile a lot.

Let's review the benefits once again:

◆ **I take much less of my own time** booking travel arrangements. The agent is a versatile travel information resource that facilitates and simplifies trip planning.

◆ **I speak to friendly, local, knowledgeable people** who have been trained to know the destination facilities and markets as a result of special certification classes, "fam" trips, and seminars.

◆ **I get the lowest current price** that my agent can find for me. When you work with your travel agent, always ask: "Is that the best you can do?" Most agents will keep on trying until they shave the cost to the lowest level.

◆ **Finally, I get on their newsletter mailing list** for monthly updates on new travel packages and destinations. By reading each issue, I find out about the latest developments in the travel industry and get information about hot destinations I may want to visit.

What's the catch? In 35-plus years of traveling on business and for pleasure, I have yet to find one. Travel agents rely on satisfied customers to spread the word to prospective new clients and expand their business base. An industry axiom is that 100 satisfied customers generate 25 new customers. If someone were to ask, I'd tell them I consider myself one of the 100.

Cost for their services? If I asked my plumber to do a favor and book a flight for me, the old geezer would bill me $60.00 an hour for his time. My CPA, $70.00. My attorney, $200.00.

My travel agent, providing the same service, charges me nothing more since she is paid a commission by the airlines and hotels. (Some agents, however, are beginning to charge a small fee for ticketing as a result of the airline commission caps). She does a much better job of trip planning than the greasy-handed plumber or the high-priced lawyer, and deserves to be paid at a professional rate.

If you like mind-numbing elevator music, keep dialing the airlines directly. But I prefer cost efficiency and convenience, so I call my travel agent and put my requirements in the hands of a pro.

The contents of this book—written by a traveler, not a travel agent—are aimed at sharing information I've learned through experience that spans four decades, to make travel more enjoyable for the reader.

Come along for the ride. But be sure to check in early.

3.

The Choice Is Change Or 'Adios'

If, of all words of tongue and pen,
The saddest are, 'It might have been,'
More sad are these we daily see:
'It is, but hadn't ought to be.'

— Bret Harte

✈ · · · · · · · · · · Ten years ago, the typical travel agent will tell you, life in the travel business was much simpler. Commissions were reasonably adequate to allow for profitability, discount services were practically non-existent, and Internet could just as well have been a gadget with which you scooped minnows from the lake. The computer was still emerging as a fascinating new business tool that quickly became a staple means of tracking prices, which changed infrequently and in an orderly way in those halcyon days.

Today, some aspects of the travel agency business have become downright ugly. A quick scan of a travel agent trade publication will reveal an industry full of conflicts, threats, and chasm-sized rifts between the agents and many of their suppliers — especially the airlines. Trust and belief in each other's adherence to sound business principles is at a low ebb, and many agents wonder if they will be able to survive long-term. The challenges on some endless days seem insurmountable.

The convulsive air fare wars have made already-ludicrous pricing structures different from day to day and from flight to flight. In our company, we not only avoid check-in blues by employing a full-time travel agent, we get the best available pricing because she spends most of her time tracking changes and fare specials.

But it's impossible to complete this chapter without analyzing the negative factors that are making some agents decide they may prefer the steamfitting vocation after all:

◆ **Schedules are almost obsolete the minute they're sent to the printer.** Each day, on average, there are over 60,000 fare changes. Someone has to track them and be aware of the latest revisions, but it's like trying to catch a single, specific snowflake out of a blizzard.

◆ **The number of resort destinations, cruises, choices of hotels** in all price ranges, and family attractions is expanding faster than anyone can comprehend.

◆ **More travelers are heading out to the more exotic destinations** without being able to access much help from the agents, who don't have time to visit even a small fraction of the new destinations that come up on their computer screen.

◆ **Couples are combining business and personal travel**, further complicating the arrangements, record keeping, and billing.

Aside from these kinds of challenges, there is a small matter of compensation (or lack thereof). A couple of years ago, Delta Airlines reduced and capped the rate of commission they pay travel agents who book tickets on Delta. Other airlines awoke from their slumber, muttered something like, "They did what?" and instantaneously followed suit with commission caps of their own.

In the first year alone, it is estimated that agents lost $700-million-plus in commissions by operating under the caps. While the airlines saved millions, many agents were forced to cut staff, reduce costs, or close their doors. Hundreds of agents closed up shop and set up agency operations in their homes (*Travel Agent Magazine*). A major class action lawsuit was filed against the airlines but less than 15 percent, or $100 million, was recovered.

And there are other challenges emerging on the horizon. For example, there's the Internet. Though currently accessed by a small percentage of the general population, online services are offering ever-improving methods to complete travel bookings on a do-it-yourself basis. Once the bugs and complications are smoothed over, and the speed of transmission is improved, more travelers are likely to look to the Internet as their source for information.

The worrisome point about the Internet, from an agent's perspective, is that many of its current users are upscale, highly-educated, substantial-income travelers — the perfect profile of a target prospect for a travel agency. Could that salient point provide a clue that may lead to transforming the enemy into an opportunity? Stay tuned.

Finally, there are the discounters who populate the radio talk shows and offer everything but the moon as a destination at heavily-discounted rates.

(Some include the moon on their menu of tours — and for the budget-conscious traveler, they're making available half-moon and quarter-moon tours at fractions of the full price).

There is no doubt that a metamorphosis is underway to re-fashion and revitalize the travel agency business and bring about much higher levels of professionalism. But while they have been cleaning up their act, the 150,000+ travel agents in the United States have encountered even more new competition that has crept into the marketplace via the Information Superhighway in recent years.

Meet the fly-by-night travel agency.

4.

Instant Entrepreneurship

*False face must hide
What the false heart must know.*

— William Shakespeare

$\dashv$ · · · · · · · · · · T he blaring "come on" is both suspicious and enticing: "FREE airline tickets." All you have to do is shell out $745.00 (normal price is $2700.00, they say) and you, too, can become a travel agent — overnight, and over the Internet.

That's the message appearing on the screen of my home computer one recent evening. And there was more:

> *"Isn't it about time YOU took advantage of this opportunity?*
>
> *"Tax breaks: All of your travel expenses may now be tax deductible. For a limited time, (company name) will allow you and a friend (program includes 2 travel agent ID cards)*

to become independent travel agents for just $745.00."

You probably noticed, as I did, the total absence of any mention of qualifications — except for a solvent checkbook. Also, the source of this message failed to note any requirement for training, capital funding, facility, or experience.

Still another organization of this type, based in Florida, has signed up some 6,000 "independent agents" at only $495 each in just two years. According to *The Wall Street Journal,* virtually anyone over 18 years of age can receive travel agent credentials with just a stroke of their check-writing pen.

Does it work? Last year alone, the Florida company booked about $20 million in commissionable sales that should have gone to legitimate agents, the *Journal* said. Similar companies that operate on the west coast have 50,000 such "agents" that gross $100 million in sales annually.

The legitimate agents who are qualified and who provide full service support to their clients are almost powerless to impede the growth of these (excuse the expression) "fly-by-nighters." But some suppliers, like hotels and cruise lines, refuse to offer their services through any unqualified and uncertified agent. To many other suppliers, the amateur agents are just another source of revenue they can't afford to pass up.

If you'd be comfortable dealing with an agent that doesn't know Schenectady from Shinola®, take the amateurs up on their "almost impossible to believe" offers. But if you have higher standards that include respect for professionalism, stick with the legitimate, local agent who is equipped and trained to provide the services you require.

Guess What? You're Hired!
No Brain Required

For airline seats, don't raise a fuss,
Just dial our number and book with us.
We're new in the business and don't know the ropes
But we get all kinds of business from all kinds of dopes.

As for qualifications, it's plain we have none
Just hand over your money and head for warm sun.
We became travel agents by paying our dues;
(It was either that or a pair of new shoes).

We'll send you away–by bus, train, or jet
But reservations are about all you'll get.
Don't ask us questions about far-off venues
We get confused by just reading some menus.

We're the new breed–the "instant agent" of today.
Our motto is, "Never let work disrupt our play."
We take calls from those in search of a good deal
And our iron-clad guarantee is made of genuine steal.

– Harry Knitter

Who knows what opportunities the next Internet message may bring? How about discounted credentials for brain surgery? Perhaps we could take advantage of their special two-for-one offer — *two med. school diplomas for the price of one . . . satisfaction guaranteed!*

Book your travel requirements with the pro's in your town; you won't regret doing business with a qualified, experienced agent who will always deliver more value than you expect — because they expect to be your agent for a long time to come.

5.

You Can't Take Internet To Lunch

If all the good people were clever,
And all clever people were good,
The world would be nicer than ever
We thought that it possibly could.

—Elizabeth Wordsworth

$\dashleftarrow$ · · · · · · · · · · So you're a frequent traveler along the Information Superhighway and you eat cyber fibre for breakfast. When it comes to planning trips, can the Internet replace your travel agent?

From personal experience, I have found the on-line services and Internet are great information sources. In fact, I did much of the research for this book through Internet rather than leaving my warm home, trudging through the slush to the East Lansing library, and fumbling through books and periodicals all afternoon. When I'm there, I also experience some of the local flavor, like the young mother who reads "Barney Loves You" to her young son at least six times per library visit. I've heard it so many times, I'm about to join the Nuke Barney Fan Club. But I digress.

The travel sections of Internet web pages are magnificent. You can access major publications like *The New York Times, USA Today,* and the *Chicago Tribune* and find out all you could possibly digest on every current travel subject. Tap a few more keys and you can be in the midst of the finest magazines and guide books like Fodor's. And other travel-related companies like American Express have extensive home pages on travel subjects.

When you're through finding all of the legitimate information, there's a section on hot deals and E-mailers who will sell you just about anything in the travel area for almost nothing if you turn over control of your credit card to them.

If you're just a plain old-fashioned traveler like me, however, the Internet will prove to be totally confusing as a reservation-maker. I'm generally computer literate, but the process of booking flights and hotels through the currently-available programs is incredibly complicated. And, if you can figure out how to work the system and actually place the bookings, you've got to enter your credit card number on line, and I'm not convinced that others can't get access to the card for fraudulent purchases.

Finally, booking flights and tips through Internet takes a lot of time. Some nights I stare at the screen for 15 to 20 minutes while the system boots, reboots, and does other strange things.

I don't know how you feel, but I vote for conversations with live people rather than computers. Your local travel agent can do all of the things that Internet does, but you get the benefit of their knowledge, talent, contacts, and other services that can make your trip successful. Comparing the two, it's important to recognize these functions that Internet travel services *cannot* perform:

◆ Establish a positive relationship that enables them to work effectively with you to help you meet your travel goals;

◆ Send you a personally-written Christmas card;

◆ Provide you with qualitative guidance on specific destinations you are considering;

◆ Give you a chance to flirt with that agent you find appealing;

◆ Provide you with the opportunity to ask all of the questions you may have on your mind without being ushered into a Chat Room

◆ Make changes in your trip itinerary without having a major collision on the Information Superhighway.

While the Internet poses a genuine threat to the travel agency business, most consumers who use it will recognize that its greatest value is dispensing information that you can use to form general conclusions — which then need to be conveyed to the travel agent who knows you and understands your needs and wants. The agent can evaluate those conclusions and convert them into a comprehensive plan for your trip.

Then they may actually take you to lunch.

Be Wary And Beware

Just a few forays into the Internet will demonstrate that scam artists are running rampant in the travel business. Super-special "deals" are available just about everywhere, and gullible customers come out of the woodwork every time the words "free" and "save" appear in print.

Here are a few tips to help avoid being "scammed":

◆ Offers by mail or phone that seem too good to be true most likely are. If you're pressured to make a quick decision, back off and spend some valuable time checking out the offer in detail before you make a move.

◆ Don't provide your credit card number over the phone unless you're absolutely sure the company behind the offer is "legit."

◆ Be extra wary if the so-called vacation trip won't take place for 60 days or more. The period of time for disputing a credit card charge is exactly 60 days. Therefore, you will have no recourse if the trip doesn't materialize.

◆ Insist on getting a street address of the company and call the Better Business Bureau for a check to see if they actually operate there.

◆ Compare prices with quotes from a professional travel agent. Even if the pro's price is higher, you'll be a whole lot better off dealing with someone you can trust.

6.

The Glass Is More Than Half Full

There are two kinds of people
in this world — those who think they can and
those who think they can't. . .
and they're both right.

— L. Spitz

There may be a few travel agents who would advise a young person entering their business to think twice about his or her decision. Competition is tough, suppliers are sometimes unfair, technology is moving so quickly it's hard to keep up, and compensation is not as good as it once was. The hours are often long and the work is frequently stressful.

They encounter some "customers" who call to request research on available flights and rates and have no intention of placing their order with the agent they're talking to. With 20 minutes of the agent's research in hand, they then call the airline and book their flights directly. Working in a travel agency can be just plain discouraging at times, some people in the business would tell you.

Then there are those who see the future through much rosier glasses. First of all, they point out that travel agents usually experience a high level of satisfaction working in a field that reaches far beyond the confines of an office. Theirs is a business that makes people happy. And, there are other reasons to be optimistic.

Take the growing travel market, for example. It is estimated that by the year 2001, tourism around the world will tally up to about $4 trillion annually in sales. In the United States, more than 25% of the population will be over 50 years of age at the turn of the century, in good health, and with tendencies (and the means) to spend more liberally on travel than the generations that preceded them. And there will be more of them than ever before in our nation's history (remember the Baby Boomer generation?).

With our average lifespan increasing each year, the senior "class" is a prime target for travel agent marketers who recognize that many prospects over 50 have money to spend, time to spend it, and a high-level desire to get around the world and see what other cultures are all about. And they don't necessarily want to vegetate on the bus and be lectured to in broken English, either. An expanding group of seniors has a penchant for exciting activities, including white water rafting, hiking, mountain climbing, and the like.

Seniors generally like group travel because they appreciate having a leader to help them move about smoothly and get answers to their questions. Also, many are single and like the idea of companionship and the opportunities to make new acquaintenances through group travel.

But seniors aren't the only homogeneous group interested in travel enjoyment. There are affinity groups and clubs for women traveling alone, singles, gays, and corporate travelers. Identifying these interested prospects and targeting a marketing campaign toward them (database marketing) should be a priority for the travel agent of the 21st century.

That's just one attribute of a new type of agent that appears to be emerging from the morass of controversy and change of the 1990's. These new "survivors" may not even be known as travel agents, but Travel Counselors or consultants who in reality are spokespeople for the suppliers providing the facilities and travel "vehicles" that make trips possible.

In a nutshell, here's what you can look for in future travels:

◆ **More professionalism** among travel agents. The amateurs, dabblers, and quick discount dealers will be history, but only if travelers are discriminating and don't accept incompetence and sloppy service — and if suppliers uphold reasonable standards in granting discounts and other privileges only to qualified, committed agents.

L. William Chiles, Chairman and CEO of Hickory Travel Systems, Inc., encourages the 10,500 agents representing Hickory to "go the extra mile for clients. Educate them on how to take advantage of rate fluctuations. Counsel them on corporate travel policies. Help them track business-travel budgets and stay within corporate travel guidelines. Enroll them in frequent flyer and frequent traveler programs."

◆ **More specialization**. In the good travel agencies, you'll be able to talk with a greater array of specialists in corporate travel, group trips, international travel, senior travel, and other areas of concentration and specialization like cruises.

◆ **Fees**. Travel agencies that are going to survive will have to apply nominal charges for booking your trip accommodations, since their low commissions from most suppliers won't enable them to continue in business. However, some of the more clever agents will wash out the fees in "packages" that might allow for rebates of the fees if you book companion reservations, or followup trips with the same firm and /or agent.

◆ **New types of communication**. Web sites on the Internet are already in use by some progressive travel agents to provide you with information regarding their services and new destination background and package offerings. I find that accessing the information available on the "Net" and then consulting with my travel agent for bookings is the best way to employ both resources.

◆ **Instant help when you need it**. Because of constantly-improving communications capabilities, you'll be able to reach your travel agent from any part of the world so they can assist you and your spouse with alternative flight bookings, deal with flight cancellations, and generally be available to serve your needs when you have problems.

◆ **Ratings of accommodations and destinations** to help find the best places to suit your needs. You'll benefit through the experience of travel agency personnel and other travelers who will critically assess the features of each destination facility and identify the winners and losers.

◆ **More conveniences**. Again, L. William Chiles: "Agents are offering additional 'convenience' services like toll free, 24-hour reservations service, assistance with visa and VAT refunds, and a network of overseas representatives and service desks."

Common Misteaks Made By Travlurs

Losing track of the time or day of your flight is one of the mistakes you'll make sooner or later if you're a typical traveler. That's the most common mistake compiled by Uniglobe Travel from their customer hot line of over 140,000 calls each year.

Others high on the list:

◆ Packing essentials like prescription drugs in checked bags rather than in a carry-on.

◆ Fighting with airline, hotel or rental car employees and making a bad situation worse.

◆ Assuming an advance boarding pass guarantees a reservation (it doesn't).

◆ Ignoring age restrictions on rental cars.

◆ Failing to check in advance about paying cash to rent a car.

◆ Discarding a hotel confirmation number.

(Source: Chicago Tribune)

Before you begin planning for your next trip, my advice to you is to take your travel agent to lunch — and find out, first hand, what's happening in the business. The information you gather will be invaluable in your planning of future journeys.

IT DOESN'T GET ANY BETTER THAN THIS

PART II

The Salad, With Dressing

7.

The Yarns
Agents Weave

There's a good time coming, boys,
A good time coming.

— Charles Mackay

$\dashleftarrow \cdots \cdots \cdots \mathrm{A}$ny travel or reservations agent who has spent a year or more in the travel business has a repertoire of stories, based on their experiences, that will keep you well stocked with smiles. Here are a few to whet your appetite:

> *The elderly lady called her travel agent to arrange air transportation for herself and her pet wire haired terrier ("Skipper") from Traverse City, Michigan to Los Angeles, California.*
>
> *Using typical agency lingo, the agent indicated that her trip would consist of several segments — Traverse City to Detroit,*

Detroit to Chicago, and Chicago to L.A. "There'll be three legs, ma'am," she observed.

"You don't understand," the lady said anxiously. "My dog Skipper has four *legs."*

*   *   *

Exasperated over the cost of his trip arrangements, one misguided traveler announced to his agent that he would forego the flight and drive instead. His destination? Hawaii.

*   *   *

An airline reservation clerk received a call from a customer who wanted to fly to "Hippopotamus, N.Y." When the agent told her that there was no such city, the traveler became irate and insisted it was a big city with a big airport. The clerk asked if it might be near Albany or Syracuse. It wasn't. Then she asked if it was near Buffalo.

"Buffalo!" she said, "I knew *it was some big animal!"*

*   *   *

The next customer wanted to fly to "Maconga." The clerk told him she had never heard of Maconga and the airline didn't fly to it. Finally the passenger pulled out his itinerary and showed it to the clerk. The destination? **Macon, Ga**.

*   *   *

Another agent's customer wanted to go to Illinois. When she asked him for the name of the destination city, he said, "Cleveland, Ohio."

*   *   *

The newly-hired errand boy of a fly-by-night "amateur" agency was sent out to the manager's car to pick up a map she wanted to have framed for her office. After he failed to return for more than three hours, the manager went out to look for him and found him sound asleep in the back seat.

Awakened abruptly, the young man brushed

*the cobwebs from his eyes, stretched, and exclaimed, "Map? I thought you sent me out here to get a **nap**!"*

In keeping with the agency's travel orientation, the boy was sent packing.

*   *   *

Then there's the passenger on a Caribbean cruise ship who summoned the headwaiter and demanded to know what time the midnight buffet would be served.

*   *   *

On a trip through several countries, a travel agent reported seeing and hearing these mis-executed translations:

A sign in Taiwan: "Welcome. Don't Enter!"

Menu item in China: "Scrambled Air."

Menu item in Yugoslavia: "Frutti Tutti ice cream."

Conversation between French women: "The women on the beach at Antibes were wearing such beautiful suit cases!"

8.

A Matter
Of Choice

In America, there are two
classes of travel — first class and with children.
— Robert Benchley

←··········· The objective is not to simply choose a travel agent. The objective is to choose:

1. The ideally-located travel agent, who is
2. best positioned to serve your needs, and
3. most compatible with your personality.

Personally, I don't care whether the travel agent is black, white, male, female, or Venezuelan. I just want to work with someone who's competent, knowledgeable about today's travel market, and with whom I can feel comfortable and develop a positive rapport.

Experts recommend that you choose your travel agent as you would a doctor or lawyer for your family. Get advice from friends and relatives who use an agent they trust.

Two of the mandatory traits of any agent I work with are accessibility and responsiveness. I don't want to have to call six times whenever I need help. If the agent is so busy doing other things that he or she is never available, forget it. By the same token, if they fail to return phone calls promptly, it's a good sign they're not interested in your business — and a good reason to find someone else who is.

My agent is always available to discuss possible travel plans and book reservations — "givens" in the field of travel agentry. But her strength is that she attends just about every travel show and presentation she's invited to — sometimes several evenings or weekends a month — and is always on top of the latest information about the newest travel packages and bargains. And, by participating in these shows, she keeps her reference base of knowledge and literature up-to-date.

If your agent doesn't do this kind of homework consistently, you're getting second-rate service for the same cost I pay for topnotch support. Knowledge — current first-hand knowledge — is one of the basic attributes you should look for in any agent you deal with.

The next most important requirement is experience. If your agent has never been sandwiched between twin Sumo wrestlers in the cramped last row of a full 727 with defective air conditioning, they won't appreciate the significance of your request to be seated in the bulkhead row up front in the economy cabin. In addition, they'll be much better equipped to recommend and book specific vacation resorts or cruises if they've been there (or at similar facilities) themselves.

The point is, they can't be totally sensitive to your needs if all they do is sit at their computer consoles all day. One of the perks of a travel agent's profession is to be able to sample many different destinations, facilities, and modes of travel, so they can understand, first-hand, the needs of their traveling clients. These are called "FAM" or "familiarization" trips.

Typically, the agents are contacted by a resort destination, city, or vacation spot and invited to tour the area and the facilities. When they arrive on the scene, the host city or facility generally makes it easy for the agents to enjoy their stays, so they'll recommend the place to their clients. But there is plenty of work to be done by the agent on site.

When my agent flew to Hawaii recently, she visited 22 different hotel venues during her weeklong stay, inspecting each one thoroughly so she could recommend the best to her clients with confidence. Did she have time to enjoy the surroundings? Of course. But she also put in substantial hours in generating information she could put to good use in helping her clients.

Travel agents often use their weekends to jet away to some destination that needs to be checked out for future referral to clients. Then they return home Sunday night or Monday to conduct their normal office businesses.

Through real-life experience on trips to a variety of destinations, a good travel agent can be much more valuable to you in booking trip arrangements. Don't be afraid to ask your agent, "Where've you been?" and expect an extensive, enthusiastic response.

When you get it, you know you've chosen well. If you're still uncertain about your choice of The agent, it's not a bad idea to find out which of your candidates is a member of the leading trade associations, Association of Retail Travel Agents or the American Society of Travel Agents. You can call ARTA at (717)545-9548 or ASTA's Consumer Affairs Office at (703)739-8739 if you need to check out the qualifications of your selected agent.

Many agents are also "graduates" of the Institute of Certified Travel Agents, where they earn certification through basic course work and professional testing. You can call (617)237-0280 to find out which travel agents in your area are Certified Travel Counselors.

Just What Do Travel Agents Do?

- Research a variety of destinations in person so they can inform you, using their first-hand knowledge, about the city or resort you plan to visit

- Arrange all types of domestic and international travel, including air and ground transportation and tour packages

- Provide assistance with insurance protection, passport and visa applications, inoculation procedures and other foreign travel requirements

- Assist in meeting planning

- Provide literature for your reference

- Conduct group tours

- Maintain customer preference profiles

- Issue boarding passes in advance

- Make travel arrangements to suit your business and travel requirements and budgets

– American Society of Travel Agents

9.

The First Key
To Success: You

'The time has come,' the Walrus said,
'To talk of many things: of shoes — and ships
— and sealing wax — of cabbages — and kings —
And why the sea is boiling hot —
And whether pigs have wings.'

— Lewis Carroll

Travel agents are capable of doing a lot of things for their clients, but mind-reading isn't one of them. Input from the customer is critically important to the agent. To set the stage for success, here are some key points to communicate early in your first conversation with the agent

- **Formulate a budget figure** in your own mind and let the agent know how many dollars you have to spend on your trip package. By communicating that information, you'll prevent the agent from laying out a trip to Rome when you can only afford a weekend at a Bed and Breakfast inn in the next county.

- **Let him or her know what destinations you're thinking about.** If you're excited about gambling in Las Vegas, you're probably not much interested in an art tour of New York galleries. At the very least, tell the agent your basic preferences — for example, whether you favor a resort location, a downtown hotel, or a budget inn.

◆ **Define your interests, likes and dislikes** so the agent can cater to your needs when they search for the perfect destination and hotel. If you're traveling with children, make that challenge known to your agent early-on in your discussions. He or she will fashion a totally different trip than if you're a senior citizen couple without youngsters accompanying you.

◆ **Provide a range of dates** if you can, so there's some flexibility to juggle schedules to get the lowest possible fares and hotel rates. Prices change as a destination progresses from one season to another and from one set of rates to another.

◆ **Establish the type of tour you prefer** and work with your agent to identify the best possible package that will maximize your enjoyment. For example, you may have always wanted to visit the homeland of your ancestors; a tour of that country for 7 to 14 days would probably be the best plan for you and your family members.

◆ **Let the travel agent know** if you have physical limitations so they can ensure your special needs will be accommodated in trip planning.

Be Prepared With Plenty Of Questions

When you give your travel agent good information, you'll receive better information in return. And once you've supplied them with your information, ask plenty of questions. For example:

1. What are my options on this trip regarding flight times, fares, optimum departure schedules, etc.?

2. Is there a penalty for changing my reservations in the future?

3. Is this the lowest possible fare?

4. What would I save by staying over a Saturday night?

5. How can I earn upgrades to Business Class or First Class without paying for them?

6. How can I order "special meals?"

Some qualified travel agents apply for and receive certification. Therefore, it is appropriate to ask,

7. Are you a Certified Travel Agent? If not, what certification have you earned?

8. Have you visited the specific locations on my itinerary? Or. . . do you know someone who has?

9. Is the location I'm heading for safe and secure? Will there be any danger in the area that I will have to be wary of or protect myself against?

By asking good questions, you'll get answers that can save you money, time, and trouble while you're enroute or at your destination. And when you use this process well, you'll probably ask yourself a bigger question: "How did I ever get along in my travels without the helpful guidance of a travel agent?

One of my "pet peeves" about travel is that I'm penalized as a business traveler by higher fares, since I can't always book my trips weeks in advance. On board, after I've struck up a conversation with one of my seat mates, I usually ask them what they paid for their seat — and invariably learn that my ticket cost several hundred dollars more.

According to Hickory Travel Systems, Inc., the discrepancy is due to the volume of changes that take place daily on air fares. Industry statistics indicate that in any given 60 seconds, airlines will make an average of 187 changes in fares. On a flight between New York and Miami, for example, one-way fares can vary between $79 to $426 for the identical class of service.

When you work through a travel agent, the agent can quickly scan what's available from all airlines on the route you want to fly (not from just one airline). . . and you wind up getting the lowest available fare. And your agent can check and recheck the fares as you close in on the departure date to see if even lower fares have become available at the time you book your flights.

10.

Your Travel Agent's Least-Known Secrets

I feel like a fugitive from th' law of averages.
— Bill Mauldin

✈ · · · · · · · · · · ·When Americans travel overseas, our behavior is often viewed with less tolerance than other nationalities. (Don't ask me why. When Swedes visiting the U.S. drink and carouse most of the night, they're called "fun-loving"; when Americans do the same in Sweden, they become known as "those drunken louts from that country with the Swollen Ego.")

To help you prepare to preserve the reputation of your fellow Yanks, here are some of the basic rules of etiquette to be observed when visiting foreign lands:

◆ **In Italy**, it is not a good strategy to eat spaghetti with tweezers. Not only will you dribble sauce all over your Pavarotti tee shirt, it will take you seven laborious hours

to finish your dinner. Of course, that's about the average length of an Italian meal anyway, so you'd be right in step with the native dining customs.

◆ **In France**, it is less than acceptable to sing a rousing rendition of the "Fighting Irish" fight song on the steps of the cathedral of Notre Dame. The humorless gendarmes will think you're trying to exploit one of their national treasures, and will likely hurl you into the Seine — where you can sing anything you want, as long as you do so underwater.

- ◆ **In Germany,** don't question the fact that many Oktoberfest beer drinking celebrations often take place in August or September. Most Germans don't pay a lot of attention to the calendar when they need an excuse to munch bratwurst, slug down sauerkraut, dance the lively Schottische, and drink beer; and, come to think of it, neither do the visiting Americans.

- ◆ **When you're involved in a cultural conversation** with a group of natives in Amsterdam about the Dutch Masters, it is not socially correct to bring up the subject of cigars.

- ◆ **When in Rome**, it is not a good idea to call Ticketmaster and demand four tickets on the 50-yard line at the Colosseum.

- ◆ **In Poland**, don't eat Czarnina (duck's blood soup) with chopsticks. Eat it with a big spoon, and keep a large stack of *quackers* at your side for munching between spoonfuls of the thick, tangy delicacy.

- ◆ **In Germany, when you hear the word "Gesundheit!,"** do not respond: *"I'm 6-feet-2. How tall are you?"*

- ◆ **When you wear a plush fur hat** with ear flaps in Russia, don't walk on country roads lined with tall hedges. You'll easily be mistaken for a Russki Raccoon and "decapped" by a Soviet marksman faster than you can say, "Double Stolichnaya, Comrade?"

- ◆ **When it rains on the plain in Spain**, wear a stylish sombrero to keep your head dry. However, remember that water will accumulate in the brim, so don't lean over abruptly to kiss a señorita's hand or you'll douse her fire of passion for you. Installing a modest down-spout would be a prudent move on your part.

◆ **When you visit Cuba,** do not plan to swim in the Bay of Pigs. Considering how those filthy rascals spend their days and realizing that they don't use deodorant soap when they bathe in slimy mud, beg off when someone says, "Last one in is a bowl of borscht!"

◆ **In Switzerland, do not attempt to yodel** robustly dur-ing the Montreux Jazz Festival. The cool dudes in attendance will conclude that you're suffering from severe pain, and some anonymous doctor in the audience will summarily remove both your appendix and your tonsils, making it extremely difficult to continue yodeling.

◆ **Avoid throwing a temper tantrum when you discover** there's no Danish on the menu in Denmark, no French toast in Paris, no Dutch treats in Amsterdam, and no Belgian waffles in Belgium. Those are terms concocted by restaurant marketers in the U.S. to confuse gullible Americans and make them think some European chefs would actually stoop to perform their culinary magic in a U.S. eatery. No way, José.

◆ **Do not use terms** like "No way, José."

11.

Tips To Know Before You Go

We live and learn, but not the wiser grow.

— John Pomfret

✈ · · · · · · · · · · As veteran trip-takers know, knowledge and experience makes travel less stressful and more enjoyable over time. Therefore, it makes sense to soak up as much information as you can before you depart, so that you can stay under control and get the most out of your travel dollars.

In the 101 Tips chapters, I'll share a wealth of experience — from the experts, as well as from 35-plus years of traveling — and help you find ways to minimize anxiety and maximize enjoyment. Here are my best shots:

Passport Renewal— There's a rule of travel (Murphy's at it again) that says anytime you get an urgent requirement to travel overseas, your passport expired yesterday. Fortunately, there's a way to apply a quick remedy to your dilemma. You call (900)

225-5674 or (888) 362-8668 if you want to get the wheels in motion quickly. Have an extra $30 ready to provide for expedited delivery.

The better way: Save the $30 and a lot of stress by renewing your passport within 12 months prior to its expiration. And, while you're at it, check to see if your spouse needs to have a passport updated.

More Than A Ticket Seller — The travel agency of today can serve as a resource. If you're planning a cruise, for example, you may plan to attend a "cruise night" sponsored by the agency where you'll meet cruise line representatives, learn about itineraries and special-interest cruises, find a cruise that emphasizes fine dining as opposed to wild partying, or that offers shore excursions focusing on wildlife observation rather than beach activities.

If you're planning a trip to Asia, check out a video about that part of the world from the agent's library. Your professional travel agent can also help with visas, health requirements, currency, VAT refunds, and local business customs.

Do-It-Yourself Dining —The airlines are serving fewer meals than we were used to a few years ago (they probably got thin-skinned about the complaints registered by passengers who would prefer C rations to most airline meals).

According to the *Chicago Tribune*, airline spending for inflight meals has dropped steadily in recent years. In the fall of 1996, for example, the ten largest airline companies in the U.S. reported an average of $4.50 per passenger in meal costs, compared to $5.25 per passenger just two years earlier, the *Tribune* found. International flights average $7.92 per passenger meal.

By contrast, Southwest Airlines, which flies only U.S. routes, spent the grand total of 22 cents on average per passenger. The no-frills airline then reflects the savings in lower airfare.

While in the airport prior to flight time, check to see if you can choose a healthful meal from a deli outlet and have it packaged so you can carry it on board. (Chicago O'Hare has kiosks near the gate areas for this specific purpose. When I discovered the deli kiosk, it was interesting to find several airline flight attendants taking advantage of the facility. They obviously knew something about airline food I had only assumed was true).

With your lunch container in hand, you'll be able to eat when you want to and — more importantly — **what** you want, rather than accepting the typical high-fat, high-sodium airline meal. This is especially helpful for diabetics and others who need special diet foods.

Guide To Fitness — If you're into fitness, plan on taking some workout clothes and equipment in your carry-on bag. Then, if you should get delayed for a long period, you can locate nearby fitness facilities, work out for an hour or so, take a shower, and resume your itinerary refreshed and ready for your cramped airline seat and dearth of activity.

To locate the best facilities for a workout, order a copy of "The Fitness Guide" by Kyle Merker from your local bookstore. It lists fitness facilities available in 45 major cities, including hotels and other locations. For direct orders, call (800) 647-0921. It's $13 by mail.

In some airports, you'll find massage and back rub services to loosen up your stiff spots and to relieve tension and anxieties.

Info. Source —The World Wide Web is a good place to go to get general travel information about your destination. But use your travel agent to book your reservations if you're serious about having a good time. (In most cases, it costs you nothing more). If you're like me, when I surf the "Net," you'll still be trying to figure out the Web address for "barf bags" when the ship leaves the dock without you.

Stretch Your Legs — When you book your flight reservations with your travel agent, ask them to reserve a seat in the emergency exit row so you'll have more leg room. If seats in that row are not available, try to switch your seat assignments when you're at the airport prior to flight time.

Once you are assigned an exit door row seat, you can usually board with the blue-bloods in first class and proceed to your seat unencumbered.

Be Prepared — Help yourself prepare for potential emergencies while traveling. In a small notebook, jot down the name and phone number of someone to call if you become ill. Also, write down the doctor's number, the dentist's number, and listings for other important contacts you might want to talk with should a problem occur.

Add your eyeglass and medication prescriptions, copies of your credit cards, and reproductions of the first few pages in your passport. Do not carry the information around with you, but leave it where you or someone else can easily access it if the need arises.

Avoid Scrambling— Keep your toiletry kit intact between trips. As a result, you won't have to search every drawer in the house for your favorite bottle of Flintstone vitamins whenever it's time to depart. Just replenish any empty containers, razor blade cartridges, etc., and you'll be ready to go when you're ready to go.

Handy Take-alongs — Veteran travelers often develop a kit of "must have" miscellany to have available when the situation warrants. Here's a list of things you won't want to leave at home:

- ◆ Extra batteries for your camera and tape player;
- ◆ Address book for postcard addressing;
- ◆ Swiss Army knife for a myriad of impromptu uses;
- ◆ Candles for those romantic evenings;
- ◆ A sink stopper if you like to take long, relaxing baths;
- ◆ Plastic bubble wrap for the daintiest of souvenirs.

Add Distinction— Prevent the possibility that someone may take your luggage by mistake from the baggage carousel. Attach something that will enable you to immediately recognize your bag and not get disoriented in the maze of confusion that reigns in the baggage claim area.

Add a decal of your favorite team's logo to the bag handle to make it instantly recognizable.

Be Ready To Wait — Prepare for waiting time in airports, since it's a certainty that you'll be spending one hour or more at each stop along the way. You will want to dress casually and wear comfortable shoes so you can do some walking while you're in a "wait" mode. Pack your carry-ons in a bag with wheels. And take along reading and writing materials, to pass the time doing something worthwhile. For additional ideas, see your local bookstore for a copy of *Holding Pattern: Airport Waiting Made Easy*, my guidebook to help make time fly when your plane doesn't. You can also get it by calling (888) 567-3363.

Take Tunes On Tapes — Invest in an inexpensive tape player with earphones so you can entertain yourself with music along the way. I enjoy taping local programs I particularly like and play "tapes from home" to give my morale a boost when I'm a long way from home. And, you can save the $3 charge for airline earphones if they are even made available.

More Waiting Tips — If you have a significant block of time to wait in the airport for your next flight, try to convince the desk clerk of the airline club of your carrier that you deserve to use the club lounge even without a membership. To begin, the holders of first class and business class tickets are normally admitted without hassle. However, coach class ticket-holders will be turned back unless you can provide evidence of special need — which can range from a health condition to a business obligation.

If you can't negotiate your way into the lounge, here are some other things you can do when your flight is delayed:

♦ **At O'Hare** International in Chicago, you can get a flu shot, attend services in a new chapel, or work on your slice at a simulated golf driving range;

♦ **In the Pittsburgh, Seattle and New York** airports, you can relieve anxieties by getting a soothing massage at the Great American Back Rub;

♦ **At the Palm Springs,** California, airport, you can relieve tension and sharpen your golf game on a putting green just outside of the terminal building;

◆ **In Seattle,** weary travelers can use waiting time to take a shower for $5, then enjoy a hair trim and manicure at the adjacent hair salon;

◆ **In the nation's newest airport in Denver**, you can visit a chiropractor; in Boston's Logan Airport, you can see a dentist; in Pittsburgh, you can get a blood pressure test while you wait;

◆ **In Miami,** the hotel adjacent to the airport terminal offers a rooftop pool, Jacuzzi, sauna, and running track for $5;

◆ **O'Hare Airport** in Chicago offers a Stranded Passenger program with cots, bedding, and blankets to help you weather delays from bad storms;

◆ If you expect a long delay **in Minneapolis**, head for the nearby Mall of America® for entertainment and shopping. After a short van or cab ride, you'll enjoy some of the most unusual attractions in North America, including UnderWater World® with 8,000 fish, amphibians, and reptiles; Camp Snoopy®, the largest indoor family theme park in the U.S. (seven acres), and the LEGO Imagination Center®, with creative model building you won't believe.

Clear The Ears — Do clogged ears during and after a flight bother you as much as they bug me? Certain kinds of flying conditions seem to make clogging more of a problem, and I'm told that people with allergies have particular difficulties. Here are some potential remedies:

◆ Swallow as frequently as you can during takeoff. If repeated swallowing causes your seatmates to strap the barf bag to your chin, try chewing gum, sipping juice or water, or nibbling on fruit;

◆ While landing, try blowing air (very gently) through your nostrils while holding your nose and closing your mouth. The resulting pressure buildup should force air back into the middle ear;

◆ If these techniques are inadequate, try to find a new product called EarPlanes® in the airport gift shop. They will regulate pressure in your ears but enable you to hear fairly normally.

Special Meals — As you make flight reservations with your travel agent, have them order special meals for your trip. When other passengers are stoking up on calories, fat, and sodium, you'll be enjoying a fruit or seafood plate, or one of dozens of other healthful choices.

Good Dining For Landlubbers — One of the best ways to find outstanding dining spots on land is to subscribe to *Food for Travelers,* billed as "the ultimate publication for those who love to travel and enjoy 'food finds.' "

A sample: "For the best in stone crabs, try Joe's in Miami Beach. Order hash browns and finish your delicious meal with key lime pie. Or waddle over to Monty's of Coconut Grove, where you can feast on all-you-can-eat stone crab."

To subscribe to *Food for Travelers,* call (312) 263-6481. With your subscription, you'll receive a free Restaurant Card good for 25% discounts at thousands of restaurants throughout the world.

You Can Never Have Too Much Current Information

One of the most worthwhile ways in which you can pass the time when your flight is delayed is to catch up on the latest news and weather information. CNN *Airport Network,* available on TV monitors in the 1,100 gate areas of about 30 major U.S. airports, provides live news, current weather information, and general entertainment programming produced specifically for the frequent air traveler.

In addition to the latest news reports, CNN *Airport Network* covers "Lifelines," with health, nutrition, and lifestyle information; "Flight Into the Future," new inventions and developments in science and technology; "Play of the Day," sports highlights; "On the Move," entertainment news and features; and "On the Money," a look at business and financial topics of interest, as well as other topics of interest to the traveler.

PART III

The Main Course

12.

Tips To Know
While On The Go

*Education is what survives when what has
been learnt has been forgotten.*

— B.F. Skinner

When the trip is at hand, it's time to use your smarts to make it an enjoyable experience, and not a nondescript blot on the picture of life. Here are my suggestions and tips to make your travels go smoothly:

Prove It — Have your picture identification (driver's license, etc.) available to prove you are who you are to the airline gate agent prior to boarding. If you don't have it, you may be turned back and not allowed to board. If you're a recently married woman, make sure your picture ID identifies you with your maiden name.

Save Time — When you board your flight and find your assigned seat, NEVER put your belongings into storage behind your seat row. If your stuff is behind you, you'll have major problems when the plane taxies to a stop and everyone jumps up to retrieve their carry-ons.

Prevent Wrinkles — Be sure to respect your neighbors' clothes in the overhead bin. Don't put your bowling ball on the Armani suit of your seat-mate and then expect it will still be wrinkle-free when you land in the new destination. (The suit may also have a wrinkle or two).

Track Your Travels — Keep a travel journal during your trip to record notes on your experiences while enroute. When you're back home following the trip, you'll treasure the memories your journal will recall and provide you with valuable reference information for the planning of your next trip.

For Better Snoozing —Take along an inflatable neck cushion so you can catch some z-z-z-z-z's on your flight without having your head slide onto the shoulder of your seat mate. On the other hand, if your seat mate is good looking, ignore this tip completely.

Keep A File — Save your ticket stubs in your original ticket jacket and file them after you return home. If your frequent flyer miles are not properly credited on your next statement, ask them for their form that will enable you to describe your trip and request the addition of the missing miles; you can easily attach the necessary information from your ticket file.

Use Good Judgment — Keep portability and practicality in mind when you invest in souvenir items. Over the years, we have passed up items like sombreros and guitars in favor of china and silverware, both of which came in portable containers, and they survived the trip without dings or breakage.

Prevent Fogging — Did you know that the effect of x-rays on film is cumulative? That means the film might not be affected if it is passed through one or two inspections, but will be fogged if it receives repeated exposure to x-rays. Hand the film to the inspector before you place your carry-ons on the moving belt.

More Than Refreshment —The typical aircraft cabin has a humidity level between 5 and 15 per cent.Therefore, your body can easily become dehydrated. The solution, obviously, is to drink plenty of liquids before and during your flight. Avoid alcoholic liquids, however, because they add to the dehydration process.

While In The Air — Get up and walk around every 30 minutes or so during every flight, to loosen your muscles and get your blood circulating. Here are additional flight tips:

Timing Is Important — As you plan your itinerary, avoid flights on Monday mornings and Friday afternoons. That's when many business travelers begin and end their weeks on the road.

There's A Difference — A direct flight is not a nonstop flight. Direct generally means that you'll have at least one intermediate stop on your flight plan.

Double-Check — When you receive your ticket, don't put it away until you have checked it carefully for accuracy in the name, date of departure and return, destination, and class. Errors should immediately be reported to your travel agent.

Prepare To Call — Prior to traveling overseas, find out the phone access code back to the United States so you will be able to get your calls through smoothly and quickly. From most parts of Europe, the U.S. access code is 001, followed by the area code and number you're trying to reach.

Don't Run Out — If you rely on medication, plan to take along more than you expect to need, in case your stay is extended. Also, take along a copy of your prescription for reference should you need it. A prescription for replacement glasses may also be a handy carry-along.

Charge — Use your credit card for most of your spending overseas. You will be billed at the most favorable exchange rate, and you'll have a detailed record of all your purchases in American dollars.

Pocket Money — Before you begin an overseas trip, contact your local bank and arrange for a small amount of currency of the country of your first destination. That arrangement will save time and reduce confusion upon arrival.

Don't Panic — If you should lose your passport, go to the nearest American consulate or embassy as soon as possible. There you will be issued documents to help you continue on your trip.

Tax Refund — When you pay Value-Added Tax (VAT) on a significant purchase overseas, ask for documentation that will enable you to apply for a refund of this tax. Usually you can turn in the documents at the airport for a full refund of the tax, but if you don't have time to turn in your documents, get the necessary form you will need to apply by mail.

Customs Comments — If you're a U.S. resident, count on declaring the total value of all goods acquired in foreign countries which are in your possession as you arrive back in the United States. You'll be able to claim an exemption of $400 per person, and be required to pay 10% duty on the first $1,000 worth of articles above the exemptions.   It's a good idea to keep all of your purchases in one bag and keep your receipts together in the same bag so that you can simplify the Customs process and save time upon your return.

Stay Calm — Avoid ranting and raving when things go wrong on your trip (no reservations at the hotel, etc.). Collect as much information as possible about the circumstances and document the problem so you can help your travel agent to solve it when you get back home and gain compensation for the SNAFU if it is appropriate.

Be sure you report it to the agent upon your return. Of course, your first move when encountering a problem is to solve it the best way you can. Ask for help from other members of your travel group if you need it.

Pay A Visit — If you know someone in the foreign town you're visiting, give them a call and arrange to visit them on their turf. An informal get-together at their home will provide you with a good idea of how natives live in that part of the world. There's much more to life in the country you're visiting than hotel rooms and cabs.

In one of my writing classes, I had the opportunity to meet Werner Richter, a professor of nuclear physics from South Africa. During a visit to Capetown, I phoned his house and let him know I was in his country on business. A short time later, his wife and son came to my hotel to pick me up and take me to their home for a barbecue dinner on their patio.

The starlit evening was wonderful, the company was terrific, and I had a unique opportunity to learn how the typical South African family lives their lives. As a followup to my trip, my new friend from South Africa is corresponding with me regularly via Internet e-mail. Travel is indeed a broadening experience.

Adjusting To Time Difference — If you're flying overnight to a destination six or more hours off your schedule, plan to stay awake until it's time for the locals to turn in for the night. For example, if you're flying west to east, sleep as much as you can on the plane and then stay up until it's the normal bedtime in the country of your arrival. Fill your day with activities so you don't nod off into a nap.

When heading east to west, don't sleep on the plane. Just stay awake and plan to go to bed at your destination's normal bedtime.

Don't Be Shocked — First-time international travelers learn shortly after checking into their hotel rooms that you can't just plug in your hair dryer or electric shaver and expect it to operate the same way as they do in your own home. For one thing, you can't even plug in your appliance because international outlets are different than ours.

Our standard two-prong plug can be used without difficulty in North America, Mexico, some of the Caribbean islands and parts of South America and Asia. In other parts of the world, you will need a converter plug and converter.

For hair dryers, curling irons, and clothes steamers, you'd be well advised to use a high-power heating converter. For shavers, computers, radios, and cam corders, a transformer type of converter should be adequate. For recharging batteries, use the high-power converter.

Check at the front desk of your hotel to determine whether

they loan out shavers and/or hair dryers that are suited to local electrical conditions. If so, you're better off keeping your appliance in your suitcase and avoiding any possibilities of damage. Frequently, the loan of an electrical device is offered at no cost or for a nominal fee.

Bumping In The Night...And Day — Few air travelers are aware that the airlines frequently overbook flights, anticipating that there will be a certain number of "no shows." When more passengers show up than the number of available seats, "bumping" occurs.

First, the airlines must seek volunteers to fly on the next available flight in return for incentives that might include free tickets,

Don't Pass Up
These Special Treats In Europe

GREAT WAY TO START: Breakfasts in European hotels are full of surprises. Although you can now walk down the street in most cities to get an Egg McMuffin®, you won't want to miss the many super-fresh treats offered in the hotel dining room. The first delight is a choice of crunchy hard rolls and breads that will house a tasty selection of jams and jellies. Then, you'll find an array of sausage, eggs, and fruits. In the Scandinavian countries, count on some choice fresh sardines, salmon, shrimp, and herring on the breakfast smorgasbord. If you're a cereal freak, you'll enjoy meusli, a combination of nuts and grains that is both crunchy and nutritious. Wash all of the good food down with tea or strong European coffee or juice, and you'll be ready to start your day the healthy way.

IF MUSIC TURNS YOU ON: If you enjoy classical music, you'll be able to overdose in Europe on some of the world's finest orchestras and soloists performing in the best-known concert halls. From Berlin's Philharmonie to LaScala in Milan, the venues are classic architectural and acoustical gems – and the audiences are serious, appreciative supporters of some of the world's great musical ensembles.

frequent flyer miles, and/or cash — plus overnight accommodations if needed. Travelers who volunteer first are chosen first.

Involuntarily bumped passengers are subject to federal regulations that apply to all but commuter flights with fewer than 60 passengers. Where they apply, the inconvenienced travelers are subject to receive up to $400 in cash, depending on the value of their ticket and the length of delay — plus hotel accommodations, meals, and long-distance phone call reimbursement.

Traveling With Children — Bring a backpack with snacks and diversions. Games, books, crayons, coloring books, or markers and drawing paper are basics. A batch of super sized postcards with stamps can create opportunities to write brief notes to friends about the trip, then walk with an adult to the nearest mailbox to mail the cards.

Small craft items, like string and beads for bracelets, help pass the time. Keep items like stuffed animals and small blankets in carry-on bags. Have drinking cups available.

You may want to consider purchasing battery-powered hand-held games to entertain kids. They take up little space, but the youngsters will find them appealing for hours.

Act Strategically — If you encounter a severe flight delay, don't elbow your way into the middle of the mob scene at the gate agent's desk. Stroll over to the nearest phone and call your travel agent for assistance. They have access to the same computer information as the gate agent, and they'll provide you with calm, personal service.

Airport Ratings — Which are the best and worst airport facilities for waiting travelers and their families? Based on my totally unscientific criteria, which include layout, convenience, scope of facilities, architectural excellence, and availability of things to do, these are my most to least favorite airports in which to spend time:

1. Chicago O'Hare — Something of everything, including "Stranded Passenger Program"
2. Atlanta — $8.5 million in artwork to view
3. Dallas — Lots of shops near the gates
4. Pittsburgh — Airmall (60 shops, restaurants)
5. Las Vegas — What else? Gambling machines
6. Seattle — The Great American Back Rub
7. Milwaukee — Brats, books, and Packer stuff
8. Minneapolis — Near the Mall of America
9. Cincinnati — Not really in Cincinnati
10. Baltimore — Smithsonian shop for souvenirs
11. Denver — New, and what a view!
12. Orange County John Wayne — Modern and nice
13. Orlando — Clean, good restaurants, pleasant
14. Phoenix — Excellent shops. Sky Harbor — great name
15. Houston International — Modern; good layout and food
16. Ft. Myers, Fla.— Easy to get in and out. Up-to-date design
17. Jacksonville — An Orlando lookalike
18. Tampa — A Jacksonville/Orlando lookalike
19. Newark—The best of the New York-area airports
20. Lansing, Mich.— Small. Modern. Convenient
21. Kansas City — Beautifully designed to minimize walking. Not many shops, though.
22. Portland — Interesting shops, modern facility
23. Ft. Lauderdale — Functional, but ordinary
24. Washington National — Conveniently located, close to the city's many attractions

25. Washington Dulles — A fair distance from town
26. New York La Guardia — Always seems crowded
27. San Francisco — Reflects the class of the city
28. Los Angeles — A good place to celebrity-watch
29. Montreal — Sprawling layout, lots of walking
30. Columbus, Ohio — Functionally designed, but nothing to distinguish it from any other airport
31. Toronto — Excellent architectural design, tacky restaurants and sculpture displays
32. St. Louis — Lots of straight concourses for walking
33. Detroit — Cramped for space, overcrowded
34. Grand Rapids, Mich. — Convenient, well-designed
35. Memphis — Good restaurants with blues music
36. Boston — Memorable only for its take-home lobster concessions, not much else
37. New York Kennedy — In need of a facelift
38. Philadelphia — Ordinary but up-to-date airport
39. San Diego — Leaves a lot to be desired. Terrible dining facilities. And they charge premium prices
40. Chicago Midway — Its only good feature is location

13.

A Little Help
Goes A Long Way

All things bright and beautiful,
All creatures great and small,
All things wise and wonderful,
The Lord God made them all.

— M. Alexander

Since I'm coping with a mild disability myself, I can get a sense of the frustration of disabled Americans who are anxious to travel like their able-bodied counterparts of U.S. society. One glimpse of the cramped bathrooms engineered into almost all jetliners tells you that disabled and wheelchair-bound travelers are in for a difficult time. And while the U.S. Department of Transportation slumbers on this issue, my local racketball club was required to install facilities for the rarely-seen handicapped racketball players. The lack of common sense in applying legislation where it is truly needed is appalling.

Of all the world air carriers, KLM Royal Dutch Airlines, SAS, Air France, Sabena and American Airlines are cited for

demonstrating the greatest sensitivity to the needs of the disabled. They provide such amenities as free storage of wheel-
chairs, personalized check-in services, and attendants who look
after disabled passengers and help them when called upon.

I particularly appreciate the early boarding policies of most
airlines which enable me to get on at my own speed before the
rest of the passengers are allowed to board. Just a couple minutes of time on the plane makes it possible for me to store my
carry-ons in an orderly manner and avoid unnecessary anxieties
while I'm attempting to get settled. Upon landing and arrival at
the other end, I wait until other passengers disembark before I
venture out of the plane and into the terminal.

Other concerns the airlines have been asked to address include the provision of extra leg room for older and disabled passengers and the universal admission of respirators on aircraft.
Another one I'd add to the list is a redesign that would make it
easier to open the packages that encase crackers and peanuts
and the small plastic bags that hold plastic silverware. I'm constantly embarrassed by having to request help to do something I
should be able to do (but can't), and opening the utensil bag is
one of life's tougher challenges for those who have limited use
of one arm or hand.

With all of our space-age high-tech capabilities, it seems
incredible that no airlines have been able to provide seating and
restroom facilities that better meet the needs of the disabled passengers who are part of their customer base.

Some travel agencies are tuned in to special programs and
group travel adventures available to the disabled and handi-

capped. If you are one of the millions of Americans who are disabled, or know someone who is, explore the special assistance possibilities that your professional travel agent can uncover for you.

14.

Pardon My Sweaty Hands

The sound of a jet, an engine warming up,
even the clopping of shod hooves on pavement
brings on the ancient shudder, the dry mouth
and vacant eye, the hot palms and the churn
of stomach high up under the rib cage.

— John Steinbeck

Although I've experienced more than two dozen overseas trips, it's still a special thrill each time I climb aboard a super-sized aircraft and jet off to some remote spot on the globe, thousands of miles from home, between fading dusk in the U.S. and emerging dawn on the European continent. There's something psychologically magical about the experience of transposing your existence, in a matter of a few short hours, from one culture to another vastly different. . . from familiar, friendly surroundings to an environment where you're suddenly a total stranger.

Even waiting in overseas airports takes on special significance. You find yourself immersed in a swirling sea of strange dialects, exotic attire, and cross-culture interaction. Simultaneously, your identity and native origin are no longer accepted at face value but questioned and reconfirmed at every step along the way. To prove you are who you are, your passport becomes your constant companion, and you rarely let it out of your grasp.

The first trip overseas was traumatic and laced with unknown expectations. My maiden European itinerary included stops in England, Finland, Sweden, Norway, Denmark, Germany, France, Italy and Spain. . . a routing dictated by a series of scheduled meetings with European distributors and dealers who sold Chrysler outboard motors. Our assignment was to present a new product line and negotiate terms of an advertising program that would be jointly funded by the distributor in each country and my company, the Marine Products Group of Chrysler Corporation.

Along with a sales associate and a representative of our U.S. advertising agency, I flew out of Metropolitan Airport in suburban Detroit on a cool Saturday evening in October 1970. The plane was packed full, and my assigned seat was in the middle of a row of three, an uncomfortable situation that helped me learn the hard way to book seat assignments strategically in the future to provide ample leg room and facilitate opportunities to get up and move around during the transatlantic overnight journey. This flight, on a cramped DC-8, offered neither.

After a long night of fitful sleep, interrupted by the consumption of dehydrating alcoholic drinks, fat-laden meals, and high-calorie dessert, we arrived in London and deplaned for a brief meeting at Heathrow Airport with the representative of our British advertising agency. We were a sleepy-eyed, disheveled trio of Americans, with ears plugged, when we were greeted by

Martin Doughty of Astral Marketing. Martin, wouldn't you know, was impeccably attired in a blue pin-striped suit and starched white shirt with a light blue polka-dot tie matching the kerchief that billowed out of his left suit coat pocket. . . typical dress for a British businessman, even on a Sunday.

During the course of a fastidiously planned hour-long meeting, we laid out strategies for the launch of our program to introduce the 1971 line of Chrysler outboards throughout Europe. Because there was no language barrier between us, Martin and our team communicated effectively, and I felt confident that our trip had gotten off to a productive start. One stop down, and only eight more to go.

At the conclusion of our meeting, the three of us expressed our farewells to Martin and climbed aboard another aircraft for a four-hour trip to Helsinki, Finland, where we were to be met by our European regional manager, Klaus Wiese. We arrived late Sunday afternoon, cleared Customs and Immigration, and shook hands with Klaus in the arrivals lounge. Because we were scheduled to be in Europe for three weeks, our baggage was considerable. Unfortunately, Klaus showed up with a subcompact-sized Volkswagen Beetle with limited space for our belongings; not to mention the three of us.

Klaus, a young German national from Cologne, was an excitable character, so his fuse box became overloaded instantly when he saw the mountain of luggage that we wheeled through the "Nothing to Declare" doorway. Having just arrived in Europe that day, we quickly learned our first European expression from Klaus, a phrase destined to be reiterated frequently during the ensuing trip: "How is this possible?"

"HOW IS THIS POSSIBLE?"

After a few minutes of lively cross-cultural haggling, we jammed our bags into his car trunk, tied several on top of the car, and stuffed ourselves inside for a one-hour trip to Hanko, a seaside town that was the site of our first dealer meeting.

We discovered immediately that Klaus was not only excitable and nervous, but that he mistook all European roads for the German Autobahn, where speeds were unlimited and unregulated. His lead-foot driving helped us to get to our meeting destination in what had to be record time. Groggy from jet lag, rumpled from long spells of sitting, and churning stomach acid from our sense of anticipation, we pulled up in front of our hotel and began to dismantle the stacks of baggage from Klaus's VW.

All we wanted to do was check in, unpack, and check out the nearest beds.

But Leo Ahlroth, the Finnish distributor hosting the meeting, had other plans. He greeted us in the hotel lobby and, in clear English, issued a persuasive invitation to join his group of dealers for dinner. If we ducked out, he claimed, the dealers would feel they were stood up by the Americans. We protested mildly, then acceded to his urging. Oh, and by the way, Leo continued, the first item on the agenda in a half hour was a group sauna. A meeting-opening sauna was apparently a Finnish tradition that he had neglected to enlighten us about earlier.

Instead of dressing for dinner, therefore, we *undressed* and prepared to meet our hosts in the sauna, bare naked. To get to the sauna from our rooms, we had to tiptoe across the main lobby of the hotel, completely nude except for the towels tied firmly in place around our hips.

The sauna (pronounced sow-na by the Finns) was a lively place crammed full of fun-loving dealers by the time we got there. About 30 sweaty men, chattering loudly in Finnish, were jammed into a cramped space designed for 20 people max. We gingerly wedged ourselves onto one of the tiered bench seats and shook hands with as many of the smiling natives as we possibly could under the circumstances, knowing that most of them didn't understand a single word of our self-introductions. As we perched on the blistering hot redwood seats, hip to hip and buttock to buttock, each of the three of us Americans had the same thought running through our minds: What in the world are we doing here, and why aren't we in a soft and cozy bed, catching up on a full night's lost sleep?

The disorienting, surrealistic experience in the sauna continued for about 20 minutes; then, without warning, the Finnish dealers started to get up and leave. Aha! We concluded that our unpleasant encounter appeared to be over, but the sense of relief turned quickly to anxiety when we found out where they were all going.

As the chattering subsided, we heard splashing sounds outside the sauna. The custom, we learned, was for the Finns to heat up their bodies in the sauna and then cool down by jumping into an icy cold pool of water. So now in a matter of seconds we were in the frigid water, shivering uncontrollably while the calm and relaxed Finns became even more animated as they chattered with each other. (If they could communicate with us, we imagined they'd be saying something like: "You Americans are really weird. You all act like you're groggy from fatigue, you stutter as you talk, your teeth are constantly clattering together, and your skin turns blue when you experience the slightest chill. What softies!")

Our tolerance exhausted, we grabbed Leo by the towel, pulled him into a corner, and said in unison: "Leo, we are t-t-t-through for the day. We're g-g-g-going to b-b-b-bed and we'll see you in the m-m-morning. What time will breakfast be served?"

He expressed disappointment that we would be skipping cocktails, dinner, wine with dinner, and after-dinner drinks just to get a few hours of extra rest. But by that time, what Leo thought was low on our priority list. Swathed in wet towels, shivering and dripping, our skin a strange purple hue, we tiptoed across the lobby, collected our keys from the head porter, and went up to our rooms for a long night's sleep. Each of us also made a mental note never to let the local distributor control our meeting agenda ever again.

One cold splash in the pool was all the education we would ever need on that subject. Unfortunately, the Finns' idea of hospitality was more than we could handle that long, tiring day.

So this is Europe.

15.

A
Forgettable Detour

This ain't the Waldorf;
If it was, you wouldn't be here.

—Notice in a country inn.
(Circa 1900)

$\bigstar \cdots \cdots \cdots \mathbf{J}$im and Barb are friends who traveled with us on some of our European group tours in the seventies. Together, we were called upon to help host groups of Chrysler Marine dealers who were sales leaders during the previous year. One year, we'd fly the winning dealers into England for a week of touring; the next, Mexico City and Acapulco; then, a boat trip up the Rhine River in Germany and visits to its magnificent castles. Playing the role of staff hosts was tough duty, we told everyone facetiously, but we "sacrificed" ourselves to let the company pay our way so we could dutifully participate in the annual company/customer ritual.

On one particular occasion, Jim and Barb were due to join our group in Switzerland after completing a series of catalog press checks in England. Because the press proofing went more smoothly than anticipated, they finished the task early and flew to Geneva, where the dealers were to arrive by charter plane a few days later. When they heard that one of our colleagues was vacationing in Rome, Jim and Barb decided to take an impromptu detour by car to the Eternal City and spend some time seeing the sights of Rome before returning to Switzerland to greet the dealers.

Jim rented a small, cramped Fiat and obtained maps of the journey south from Geneva, through France and Italy, and on down to Rome. During the processing of his rental agreement, Jim casually asked the clerk how long the trip by car would likely take.

The agent glanced at the maps, scratched her head, peered at the clock and said, "Seex hour, Monsieur. . . maybe — 'ow do you say? Eight." So, armed with that time estimate, the neophyte European Road Warriors were soon on the way.

They learned in the first 50 kilometers that the Alpine roads in Switzerland, for the most part, go up and down, rather than north and south or any other direction. Making their way slowly on the narrow two-lane roads, constantly shifting gears and frequently thumping on the brake pedal, Jim discovered that after six hours of stressful, tiring travel they had barely progressed on their journey to Rome.

Already experiencing fatigue, they decided to stop for dinner in a small village at the base of a mountain. It was no surprise to find the menu was in French, the staff spoke only French, and the natives were predictably surly about accommodating a couple of drop-in Americans who couldn't tell whether they were eating a slimy eel delicacy cooked in rich wine sauce or the tongue of a young calf that had been run over by a Citroen. Jim recalls vividly that the wait staff's mood throughout the meal could be summed up in one word: rude. They all acted like they had swallowed a sour cod for lunch.

With a less than satisfactory mystery meal under their belts, they resumed their trek south. Daylight had been slowly drained out of the sky, so they were now challenged by pitch black darkness, accented by heavy fog at the higher elevations, narrow roads, and steep dropoffs with no railings at the side of the roads. Guiding the unfamiliar stick-shift car uneasily around the hairpin turns, Jim became increasingly concerned for their safety, so they decided to look for a hotel. By this time, ten hours of their "seex-hour" trip had elapsed, and their maps showed they were still many kilometers from the fountains of Roma.

Several quiet villages came and went and no hotels were to be found. Finally, in a quaint Alpine valley, Jim spotted a flashing sign he interpreted as a hotel marker and pulled the car up near the main entrance. Bouyed by this discovery, he entered the tiny office and pleaded his case for a room. Holiday Inn it wasn't, he concluded quickly.

The innkeeper, in broken English and fluent French, said, "I will show you zee bed, Monsieur." To Jim's surprise and bitter disappointment, the so-called bed turned out to be a pile of moist straw in an open barn. The scene was literally that of a manger. Some bent cart wheels and bits of broken carriages littered the floor of the barn. It would not have been surprising, Jim recalls, to have three wise men show up at the door bearing gifts. Desperate as he was, he rejected the sub-standard accommodations, explained the situation to his stressed-out spouse, and started up the car for a resumption of their nerve-rattling trip. Up and down. Down and around. Up and down.

After a while, spirits sagging and lacking in knowledge of exactly where they were, the wayward couple arrived in a small town called Gap. It was around midnight, and they were both exhausted, so they accepted the room without a prior inspection. The mattress of their bed was thick and soft and the springs were weak; so when they climbed into bed, the mattress formed a "V" shape and they were squashed together in the middle of the bed. But the tiring events of the day caused them to quickly doze off and sleep soundly.

In the morning, now nearly 24 hours after they had departed Geneva, the Americans headed for the Mediterranean coast of France. Their route took them through the scenic wine country, where farmers tend to their vines on the sides of steep hills without the benefit of mechanized equipment. In some of the vineyards, donkeys negotiate the steep grade of the hills to haul equipment and harvested grapes.

Around the middle of the day, Jim and Barb arrived on the seacoast, where they were welcomed by a beautiful vista that featured the green-blue hue of the ocean, frosted by the foam of gentle waves rolling in toward shore. Sensing an opportunity to create a positive turn to the trip, Jim parked the Fiat at a charming restaurant on the sea shore and negotiated a table that overlooked the Mediterranean.

Sipping French wine and gazing at the stripes of sun over the shimmering surface of the azure sea, Jim observed that the setting was one of the most beautiful they had ever witnessed in their life together.

Barb, on the other hand, failed to capture the rapture. Her response was as surprising as it was emotional. Mopping tears· that were streaming down her face, she said, with voice quivering, "What are we (sob) doing here? We have a (sob) beautiful home and two beautiful (sob) children, and here we are in a strange country, where we're foreigners, and we don't know where we're going and . . . why are we (sob) punishing ourselves like this?"

As a sailboat glided silently over the surface of the ocean in the distance, Jim took her hand in his, wiped a tear from her eye, and replied, "Hon, there are millions of people in the world who would pay a king's ransom to be where we are. So how can you feel so miserable? This is paradise to most people."

His unconvincing words had an immediate effect on her emotions. She burst into tears all over again and took off for the car. A couple of minutes later, now 28 hours into their six-hour trip, they were back on the road to Rome. Ah, the worst of this episode is behind us, he thought.

To prove his early experience had taught him nothing, however, he delayed their search for sleeping accommodations until after sundown and found none. Therefore, faced with a dearth of options, they decided not to try their luck in finding a hotel. Instead, they elected to bed down in the cramped Fiat.

While Jim thought he had positioned the car on a quiet street, out of the way, they found out the hard way that they were actually blocking an alley way which was used in the early morning

hours each new day by a lineup of trucks that transported veg-
etables, fruit, poultry and other livestock to market in Rome. At
daybreak, then, the two unsuspecting Americans were abruptly
awakened by truck drivers who tooted their horns and pounded
on the car windows to rouse them from their fitful sleep. A few
Italian curses were hurled their way for good measure before
Jim started up the engine and moved the car, leaving a small
crowd of angry truckers in their wake.

   They continued their journey south, arriving in Rome during the morning rush hour. Completely confused by the traffic
circles, the legions of fast-moving cars, and the mix of bikers
and motor scooter maniacs interspersed in traffic, Jim and Barb

had new reasons to fear for their lives. As they proceeded cautiously through the congested traffic, they couldn't help feeling that the Italian drivers must wear out the horns on their cars long before they wore out their brakes.

Finally, after many stops for directions, Jim wheeled the car into the rental car parking lot, checked it in, and proceeded to the airport for a flight back to Geneva. No friend. No tour. No Roman holiday.

Their six-hour trip had taken them two and a half days.

And used up about two gallons of tears. Looking back on the adventure, Barb felt much better now that it was over. After all, she reasoned, there were 2-1/2 less days until they would return home.

16.

White Knuckles On The Autobahn

Fasten your seatbelts. It's going to be a bumpy night.
— Bette Davis

✈ . . . . O ur destination was the Dom Hotel in the heart of downtown Cologne, Germany. How we got there alive was a miracle.

We traveled from Chicago to Zurich, Switzerland, on a charter flight with a group of 50 or more marine dealers and their spouses. They were going to spend a week in Switzerland as a reward from the company for volume sales during the previous year. Once we reached Zurich, my wife Nancy and I and another couple — Connie and Pete of Ross Roy, our advertising agency in Detroit — were planning to go on to Cologne, where we were scheduled to meet with our German agency.

The charter flight went smoothly, and we arrived in Zurich more or less on schedule. That was the only phase of our trip that went normally.

When we checked on the status of our flight to Bonn-Cologne airport, we found that area to be socked in with fog, and the nearest open airport was in Dusseldorf, about 100 kilometers from Cologne. So, with no real options, we soon boarded and got on our way to Dusseldorf.

The fog was spreading through Germany, but our plane slipped under the overcast and landed in Dusseldorf without incident. The problem now was to figure out how to get to Cologne. Pete and I caucused briefly and agreed to split the fare for a cab ride, which would set us back about $100 apiece. Since the hour was getting late and we hadn't slept since we left the States, the decision to hire the cab was a "no brainer".

The four of us, plus a substantial heap of luggage, wedged into a small Mercedes taxicab, and our driver set out for Cologne on the German Autobahn, which is famous for its high-speed driving (there's no speed limit). It hadn't occurred to us, however, that the same fog that socked in the Cologne airport was also challenging drivers at ground level. A little fog never phased a German taxi driver, however.

We made our way toward Cologne at about 90 miles an hour in conditions that limited visibility to less than six feet. To add to the surrealistic setting, the driver tuned his radio to a political broadcast in which the speaker was delivering an emotionally charged address like the German equivalent of a Louis Farrakhan speech.

To summarize, then, let's review the conditions:

◆ Fog the density of homemade sauerkraut

◆ Bullet-like speed

◆ No leg room

◆ Less hip room

◆ A German radio commentator blasting the party in power; or any party that came to mind

◆ A driver who didn't understand a syllable of English.

With special intercession from the heavens, we avoided several opportunities for a massive collision and somehow made our way to Cologne, where we encountered still another challenge: how to find the Dom Hotel. The driver, we reminded ourselves, was from Dusseldorf and was as familiar with the streets of Cologne as he was of Hackensack, New Jersey.

He drove around aimlessly for a while, occasionally uttering a few Germanic guttural sounds that could only have meant "Why did I have to get myself involved with this bunch of bleeping Americans when I could be home watching a Rin Tin Tin movie, with Arnold Schwarzenegger?" Finally, he spotted a group of local pedestrians at a bus stop and pulled over to the curb.

When we arrived on the scene, conversation was non-existent. About five minutes later, however, after the driver had asked for directions to the Dom, every one of the 10 or so people waiting for the bus became embroiled in a heated argument with someone else. The topic of their discussion, of course, was the optimum route to the Dom Hotel . . . and no two people agreed on the same course of action.

Having gleaned enough information from the group, the driver climbed back into the cab and drove us about two blocks to the front entrance to the hotel. We unloaded our bags, paid the driver, and checked into our rooms for a well-needed rest.

If we had opened the windows and listened carefully, we probably could have heard the massive argument that was in progress over at the bus stop.

Had we done so, we probably would have wondered what the shouting was all about.

17.

Befuddled
In Bruges

Now and then
There is a person born
Who is so unlucky
That he runs into accidents
Which start out to happen
To somebody else.

— Don Marquis

It began innocently enough. Lou, who had served as a U.S. Infantry Forward Observer in the Italian Alps during World War II, wanted to visit some of the famous Belgian battlefield sites. He and business colleague Jim were in Bruges, Belgium, to attend a horticultural conference. They had a free day before the event began, so they got together and decided to drive into the countryside in Jim's rented Volkswagen.

After Lou and Jim had finished breakfast in the hotel dining room, they strolled out the front door of the Bruges hotel. Escorting his gimpy-legged boss to a nearby bench, Jim suggested, "Why don't you wait here, and I'll run and get the car and pick you up in a few minutes?" Lou nodded his agreement, since Jim's gesture would save a couple of blocks of walking that would have made Lou's aching knees even more trouble-some than anyone suspected.

Jim hurried to the underground parking garage where he had left the car the day before. After paying the attendant, he steered the VW cautiously into a one-way street that paralleled one of the many malodorous canals that ran at a moderate pace through the city centre. As in many European cities, the streets of Bruges fanned out from the city centre like spokes on a bi-cycle wheel.

Once on the one-way street adjacent to the parking garage, Jim realized that he couldn't immediately turn back toward the hotel because of the canal. So he drove on, looking intently and eagerly for a bridge that would enable him to make a left turn and cross over the canal. He believed that by getting to the other side, he would be able to reorient himself and find the hotel. . . where Lou was seated on the bench, waiting patiently for him to return.

By this time, however, Jim was not only hopelessly lost, he was totally devoid of any conception of direction. Maneuvering the stick-shift VW slowly, carefully along the narrow street, bumping along on the cobblestones, he turned in the general direction where he thought the hotel was.

Spotting a group of tourists walking toward a covered bridge, Jim turned in behind them and headed toward the bridge at a slow speed. Halfway across, he encountered a large steel pole in the center of the roadway that was located there for a single reason — to prevent vehicles from using the pedestrian covered bridge.

He then had to back up into the one-way street with the

taunts of the tourists ringing in his ears and resume his "progress" toward the hotel. At the corner, he turned left in the general direction of where the hotel was located, according to his unscientific calculations.

Unfortunately, the turn brought him to an intersection that was lined with people anticipating the arrival of a holiday parade commemorating the war. Thinking he could beat the parade, he turned quickly into the street, only to discover that he was directly behind one of the marching bands. The parade order of march didn't, regrettably, call for the addition of a confused American bucking and jerking along in an undecorated VW. There were colorful and noisy bands and marchers in front

of him and bands and marchers behind him... and he couldn't see any way to extricate himself from the line of march because of the confounded canals to the left and right as he inched along. At this point, his entire body was soaked with perspiration, and it became difficult to see because of the annoying droplets of sweat that were cascading off of his forehead and into his eyes, causing vision blurring and a burning sensation deep inside his eye sockets.

After what seemed like hours, he finally found an opening in the parade crowd and made a sharp left turn, heaving a sigh of relief as he slowly cleared the parade route. At one point, because of the congestion surrounding the parade event, he had to drive on the sidewalk to get to the next thoroughfare. As he moved at a gingerly pace toward the next intersection, he steered around a woman who was carrying a bag of freshly-baked French bread. She took the opportunity to display her extended middle finger for him and shout profanities in Flemish while he smiled weakly and shrugged his shoulders. He assumed correctly that she was not signaling that he was Number One in her heart.

Suddenly his attention was captured by the dreadful discovery that the VW was on yet another one-way street — and, as his heartbeat began to accelerate once again, he found that the car was pointing south and the directional signs were pointing north.

The observation was just what he didn't need. Here I am, he thought, I'm totally lost, unable to communicate with anyone around me, and now I'm breaking the law. What kind of disaster could possibly happen next? he thought.

Then he found out: a Bruges police car was parked on the

next corner. The gendarme was standing in Jim's path, and he had no choice but to stop and climb out of the car.

Since Jim spoke no Belgian, nor Flemish, nor anything other than English, and the traffic cop spoke no English, the American was consumed by total panic. In desperation, he opened his billfold, took out a $20 bill, and waved it in front of the policeman's face. The cop was not amused and began to shout at Jim in a flurry of foreign words and phrases that, loosely translated, instructed Jim that he was on the verge of being arrested for attempted bribery of a police official.

Having listened to a lengthy lecture in Flemish on the rudiments of Belgian driving, Jim finally got back on his journey to the hotel. Arriving at the front entrance a few minutes later — only three hours after he had left — Jim parked the car at the curb, got out, closed the door, and stretched both arms on top of the car, cradling his perspiration-soaked face. In a moment, he heard Lou Brand approaching.

Lou opened the car door, sat down in the front passenger seat, closed the door, took off his sunglasses, tightened his tie, cleared his throat and observed, "Looks like we may get some rain, Jim."

18.

A Simple Matter Of Time

Time driveth onward fast,
And in a little while our lips are dumb.
Let us alone. What is it that will last?

—Alfred, Lord Tennyson

✈ · · · · · · · · · ·Shari is a friend and gregarious business associate who travels incessantly. At the drop of a briefcase, Shari is on his way to the airport, heading for who knows where? Often his "who knows where" is a distant dot on the globe — some exotic European capital like Vienna, where his brother resides, or the bulging city of Teheran, where he grew up and gained his basic education before coming to the US to earn a number of degrees, including his doctorate at Michigan State University.

Shari is not only a frequent flyer, he's a frenetic traveler who seems to have trouble find him even though he never starts out looking for it. During a recent trip to South Africa, for example, he was with us in the airport terminal one minute and, in the next second he had vanished. My boss and I frantically searched the terminal as flight time approached, and we couldn't find him anywhere. Then, after resolving not to leave Capetown without him, we stumbled across him in a remote corner of the airport, redeeming a huge stack of his Value Added Tax receipts for refunds—with about 10 minutes to go before the scheduled departure of our 15-hour flight to Miami.

But the story about Shari that stands out most vividly in my memory involves the first leg of a planned trip from our home airport in Lansing, Michigan. The itinerary called for his departure at 1 p.m. from Lansing to Detroit, a 30-minute hop.

After a layover in Detroit, he would board a 5:40 flight to Amsterdam, Holland, and continue on to Zurich, Switzerland, his ultimate destination. Because he had recently experienced a problem with the 1 p.m. flight and knew that it was often canceled, Shari decided to be extra cautious and book the 10:40 a.m. flight to Detroit, figuring that if the hopper would be canceled for some reason, he'd still be able to get on the 1 p.m. flight and arrive in Detroit with plenty of time to catch the Amsterdam plane. His reasoning seemed logical enough.

However, if you've traveled even a little bit, you can almost predict what happened next. The clock in the terminal struck 10:40, and nothing happened. The same phenomenon occurred at 11:40 and 12:40, at which time the airline announced the 10:40 flight was canceled.

A similar sequence of events occurred with the 1 p.m. flight as the airline experienced every known mechanical difficulty. . . and some obstacles never before encountered. The airline agent, Dave, had arranged for limousine service, but cancelled the limo when he received a premature report that the plane was ready for boarding. Meanwhile, Shari was devouring stomach tablets and biting his nails incessantly. And eating. Cookies, hot dogs, candy bars, anything that even faintly resembled food. Finally, at 4:40 p.m., the plane was reassembled, the passengers were boarded, and the aircraft was prepared to depart from the gate. A mild cheer erupted in the cabin when the plane finally began to move.

While in the air halfway to Detroit, Shari calculated his arrival in the Motor City would be within 30 minutes of his scheduled departure to Europe. Since he was quickly running out of time, he summoned the flight attendant and arranged to have a porter and golf cart waiting in Detroit to whisk him on his way through the airport terminal to his departure gate. . . which, of course, would be at the opposite end of the airport from his arrival gate.

That task having been accomplished, he gulped down a couple of stomach relaxers and sat back to catch a glimpse of southeast Michigan landscape while the pilot lowered the flaps and prepared to land at Detroit Metropolitan Airport.

A few short minutes later, the aircraft was on the ground, taxiing toward the gate. The passengers readied their carry-ons for a quick transition into the terminal, since 100 per cent of them were running hours late. At long last, the aircraft taxied to the gate and stopped. Everyone on board jumped up out of their seats, emptied the overhead bins and waited for the door to open their way to the terminal. Shari stood on the seat to reach his flight bag and climbed down facing the exit door. Then he waited. And waited. And waited. It was now 45 minutes and counting to the Amsterdam departure. 40. 37. About 35 minds shared a common thought: "What's holding that @#$%&*#@ door?"

Finally, the long-awaited announcement from the captain: "Ladies and gentlemen, we've been told that we inadvertently parked a bit off center on our designated mark, and they can't get the jetway to operate correctly. Therefore, you'll have to return to your seats while we restart the engines and maneuver the plane to the correct spot. We apologize for the inconvenience."

If thoughts could kill, the pilot would have been on his way at breakneck speed to shake hands with St. Peter. Now there were 19 minutes to flight time.

Finally, the missing "spot" was located, the engines shut down, and soon people were shoving their way down the aisle toward the jetway. And, oh yes. They were also shaking their fists at the errant pilot as they deplaned. A few signaled to him that he was number one.

Shari was one of the first passengers up and out, on his way to the waiting porter and golf cart.

Uh, oh. No porter. And no golf cart. He quietly muttered something philosophical to himself in Farsi. And he started to perspire. Gate 97A, here we come.

With just a few minutes to go, Shari started sprinting toward the distant gate, with briefcase and clothes bag flailing about in all directions as he pumped his short legs and huffed his way down the concourse. *9 minutes to go.* His chest burned and his head ached with pain.

At the opposite end of what appeared to be an endless tunnel, he could barely see the faint image of a gate agent peering down the corridor for late-arriving passengers. Legs stiffening and sweat pouring from his forehead, Shari could now make out the sign that read "Gate 97A" and began to feel confident that he could, indeed, make the flight.

But what he felt would not come to be. For the gate agent standing in the aisle was signaling him to slow down because the boarding door had been closed, and the flight, for all intents and purposes, had left the gate seconds earlier.

"I've got to be on that (bleeping) flight!"Shari roared as he approached the gate area. His chest was heaving as he huffed and tried to catch his breath, but he had enough oxygen left in his lungs to shout, "Call them and have them open that door!"

He added a few Farsi holy words for effect.

With the most arrogant of smirks on her face, the gate agent declared, "Sorry 'bout that. You were supposed to be here two hours before flight time. When you arrive at the last minute, you run the risk of missing your flight. The aircraft is taxiing to take off."

The demeanor of the gate agent was far too sanctimonious for any rational being to bear after all Shari had been through. At this point, he lost his composure, and simultaneously lost his footing on the slippery tile surface. In an instant, he was sprawled out on the floor, and his briefcase was inadvertently sent flying toward the agent while Shari was spewing Iranian threats and expletives in all directions. Papers and belongings were scattered about as the gate agent ran to a phone to summon emergency support. Within seconds, security guards surrounded Shari as he tried to regain his poise and explain his sudden loss of control. And then, miracle of miracles, the plane suddenly appeared once again at the gate, the door was begrudgingly opened, and Shari was ushered onboard the aircraft.

With sweat pouring out of every pore, he stumbled down the aisle, clutching his half-empty briefcase and his rumpled clothes bag, until he found an open seat, where he parked himself and his carry-on luggage.

His chest heaved, and perspiration dripped from his face. He tried to compose himself while hundreds of eyes observed his every move. But, despite his discomfort and his emotional state, he was, after all, on his way to Zurich.

It was simply a matter of time.

If you knew Shari, you would anticipate hearing another episode when he returns from his next trip.

There's the time, for example, when he was caught by customs agents with baking soda in a plastic bag for brushing his teeth. A plastic bag with white powder. We'll save the story for the next time we meet....

19.

And Where Exactly Is First Gear?

Strait is the gate, and narrow is the way, which leadeth unto life, and few there be that find it.

— The Bible

✈ · · · · · · · · · · Cindy and Lou (he's my company's chairman of the board) graciously invited my wife Nancy and me to be their travel mates for a trip in 1991 to Rimini, a seacoast town in northern Italy, where we were to attend a horticultural business meeting. As we prepared for this experience, my blood pressure racheted up a notch or two when I learned that it would be my role to debut as a European driver, at the wheel of a rented Volkswagen van toting our foursome and about a half-ton of luggage between the small airport in Forli, Italy, and the conference location in Rimini. The 35-mile trip represented too much distance to hire a driver or taxicab, so the responsibility for a safe journey from airport to hotel rested firmly on my quivering shoulders.

Since I was incapable of comprehending more than 14

words in Italian (most of them relating to pasta entrees), I anticipated early on that I would be at a distinct disadvantage on the unfamiliar Italian highways and narrow city streets. After all, my primary education on northern Italy had been a couple of Sophia Loren films I saw in my teen-age years — and I must admit I wasn't thinking about highway signs while my eyeballs were glued to Sophia.

What's more, as you might anticipate, my party of three equally apprehensive and unknowledgeable passengers would prove to be of little help . . . and even less moral support.

Our long and tiring flight from the States to Frankfurt, Germany, and on to Forli, was smooth and uneventful. But from that point on, a double dose of anxiety set in, and our real adventure began. As we entered the terminal, I headed straight for the Hertz counter while my travel comrades took off for the nearest "toilettes" — to ingest a strong helping of Valium, I suspected.

At the rental counter, I began to deploy my narrow vocabulary of Italian words and phrases, none of which made any sense to the counter agent. (He was wondering to himself what pasta had to do with my desire to rent a vehicle). Finally, I rummaged through my briefcase and produced a written confirmation of my rental car contract spelling out the terms of our van requirements. With arm flailing, the counter agent — who knew about 13 English words — explained to me that all was in order except for one minor detail. It seems the senior Hertz agent had needed a vehicle to transport her to lunch and had decided that our van suited her needs. At that moment, therefore, our options were somewhat limited — we waited.

I should say, *I* waited. Lou headed back to the toilette, and the ladies went shopping for discount Italian leather. After 12 hours of overnight travel from the US, we were more than slightly perturbed with the AWOL agent. However, we realized that any complaints we could register would be relatively ineffective considering our language limitations.

Eventually, the errant van came roaring around the turn and peeled rubber into the parking lot, leaving clouds of dirt and fumes in its wake. The lunch had obviously been consumed and the wine glasses drained, and the agent was ready to do business. In a couple of minutes, the rental agreement was signed and we were on our way, armed with directions carefully but emotionally described by the senior agent, who knew 12 words of English. Finally, we bolted through the parking lot exit, the VW bus performing like a bronco from Wyoming while I relearned how to operate a stick-shift transmission. Finding first gear was my first positive accomplishment.

A short distance from the airport, we encountered a toll booth and a sign indicating that the road to Rimini was 180 degrees in the opposite direction from the route I had been instructed to follow by the senior rental agent. My three nervous American navigators — one a former military forward observer in WW II — insisted vehemently that I turn the bus around and follow the sign. With equal vehemence and control of the steering wheel, I ignored their pleas and decided to follow the Hertz routing. My sweating palms caused my hands to slip on the wheel as I turned the van onto a highway entrance ramp and continued our journey to who-knew-where.

For the next 50 kilometers or so, silence reigned as all four of us strained our eyes to read the infrequent signs, attempting to identify clues as to where we were heading. To everyone's amazement, we spotted an exit sign marked "Rimini" and coasted down the ramp to the toll booth — where we relieved our bill-folds of a couple of hundred lire in tolls. A second sign, just beyond the toll booth, read "Il Mare." With five years of high school and college Latin under my belt, I loosely translated the sign to mean, "To the Sea, Dummy!" and we turned left toward "Il Mare" — since we knew that Rimini was on the Adriatic seacoast.

A few kilometers and a couple of gear-grinding downshifts later, we spotted the sign on our hotel. Actually, my backseat passengers noticed the sign, since Lou and I were busy catching a few glimpses of the topless beach inhabitants on the right side of the road. With a half dozen deft maneuvers, I wheeled the bus squarely into the entrance to the hotel driveway where, I had hoped, we could unload our massive collection of heavy baggage. To our dismay, however, the drive up to the lobby entrance was lined by two dozen or more luxury cars. Mercedes, Porsches, and BMWs on the right. Audis, Lexus, and Jaguars on the left. And, in the middle, space between the two rows that was equal to the width of our VW bus plus a millimeter or two.

"You won't make it. Don't even try," the boss proclaimed authoritatively.

"It's too narrow, " Cindy chimed in.

"Forget it," Nancy advised.

"Naw, there's plenty of room," I responded stubbornly, the perspiration on my palms increasing as my blood pressure shot upwards. To assert my confidence, I revved the engine and the van vibrated violently. Once again, I fumbled around for first gear, which was nowhere to be found.

I inched the van forward, releasing the clutch carefully and holding the steering wheel tightly. We edged forward into the driveway, meter by meter, until we heard a sound that vaguely resembled a scraping sound. Then, a crunching sound. Metal to metal. Then the sound of my quivering voice:

"I'm stuck. It's too narrow. I can't make it through," I admitted sheepishly while my passengers stared at each other quizzically.

The task at hand, at this awkward juncture, was to extricate myself from my self-caused predicament. We were stuck on the left side, and stuck on the right side.

I fumbled with the gear shift lever, clumsily and frantically trying to locate reverse gear. Letting out the clutch a small bit at a time, I coaxed the van to move backward, ever so cautiously.

With a couple of scratching and scraping sounds for good measure, we freed ourselves from the multi-vehicle vise and I parked the bus at the end of the driveway.

As we walked up the road toward the lobby, the Boss advised, "Don't look at the damage; someone may be watching us from their room in the hotel. Look straight ahead and pretend nothing happened."

Actually, nothing did happen. As I casually glanced at the cars lining the driveway, there wasn't a single sign of any damage. Nothing on the Audi. Nothing on the Mercedes. Nevertheless, we continued walking straight to the hotel, chatting informally as if everything was cool. The problem, it turned out, sounded much worse than it actually was. We were justifiably relieved.

Finally arriving at the front desk after our long journey, we wanted to check in, get our baggage settled, and enjoy a long night's rest. But the desk clerk would have none of it. His message? "We are out of rooms. You'll have to stay at our annex hotel on the next street. Just bring your car up the driveway of this building and a porter will take your baggage to the other hotel."

With one subtle wink, and without cracking a single smile between us, Lou and I said in unison: "Why don't *you* take the keys and bring our van up the driveway so we can drop off the baggage?"

With a smile and a nod, the porter went on his way. In a few minutes, we heard scraping sounds out on the driveway.

Metal to metal.

20.

Anyone For Lemon?

One may not doubt that, somehow, good
Shall come of water and mud
And, sure, the reverent eye must see
A purpose in liquidity.

— Rupert Brooke

✈ · · · · · · · · · · W̲hen I told him that I was writing this travel book, Dr. Kenneth Marton, my optometrist, described his first overseas trip to the Far East. He was on a speaking tour of seven countries, the first of which was South Korea.

His long transcontinental flight went smoothly, and everything seemed to be in order until he arrived at the Seoul airport, when he found that the Korean host who was supposed to pick him up and take him to his hotel room was a no-show.

The time was now near midnight on a Sunday, and all airport shops were closed. So he gathered up his luggage and headed out the door, following arrows pointing to the currency exchange bank. When he got there, it was closed, of course.

He tried to get back into the terminal to exchange his American currency but was met at the sliding doors by two military guards with guns drawn. Whoops! Let's try the taxi stand, he thought to himself.

There, none of the cabbies understood him when he tried to pronounce the name of his hotel, so he went down the line of cabs until he found one driver willing to take him into town. Once in the cab, he showed the driver the trip itinerary form furnished by his travel agent, the driver nodded and bowed, seemingly in tune with the name and address of the hotel.

When they drove out of the airport complex and approached the first stoplight, the engine of the cab died.

But, after several cranks of the ignition, the cabbie got it started once again and chugged his way toward the city. Once in town, he seemed to choose the very worst, ugliest neighborhoods to traverse on the route to the hotel.

Now almost totally exhausted from tension of his long trip, as well as jet lag, the doctor dozed in the back seat, with a sense of comfort that he was at least making some small progress toward his destination. In the middle of one of the worst neighborhoods, however, the taxi chugged for the last time, the "overheat" light came on, and the engine died.

The driver coasted over to the curb, got out of the cab, and raised the hood, looking very confident that he could discern the problem quickly, fix it, and get them back on their way.

Not so easy.

It seems the problem was engine overheating caused by a leaky radiator hose; the temporary solution was that they needed water for the radiator.

It was now about 2 a.m. and the street was deserted. The

driver boldly marched up to the first doorway he found and started to pound loudly on the door to awaken the occupants of the run-down house. To the driver's surprise, the door opened after a few moments, and a little lady listened to his description of their dilemma.

The door shut, and the cab driver remained on the steps as if transfixed. After a few minutes, the door reopened, and the lady handed the driver a teapot full of water.

At that moment, Dr. Marton awoke from his brief nap.

Here he was, in the middle of Seoul, Korea, totally lost, seated in the back seat of a rundown taxi, watching his cab driver pour liquid from a teapot into the cab's radiator.

"Is this an omen?" he asked himself. It wasn't.

They were soon on their way, although the taxi kept stalling every few blocks, and he eventually made it to the hotel.

But for the generosity of a little Korean woman, he'd still be sitting in the midst of a slum somewhere in the outskirts of Seoul, wondering whether he'd ever be home again. As it turned out, he got to his hotel safely and, a day later, got to deliver his presentation, titled, "Creative Remedies for Sports Eye Injuries."

PART IV

The Dessert

21.

Tips To Know: The Afterglow

There was a young lady named Bright
Whose speed was far faster than light.
She set out one day
In a relative way,
And returned home the previous night.

— Arthur Buller

┼ · · · · · · · · · · ·While you're settling down in your normal world back home following your trip experience, take some time to pull the pieces of your trip together so you can savor the happy moments of your travels and share them with friends and family. Get your pictures processed promptly and put them in easy-to-use photo albums so you don't wind up digging through drawers and trying to remember the sights and events of your trip ten years after the fact.

I've always found it a good idea to contact my travel agent shortly after arriving home, thanking them for the positive things that happened and discussing any shortcomings of the travel arrangements they made for me. If you had problems, let them know immediately so they can take corrective action with the source of the difficulties. Before you start firing off letters to

143

hotels and restaurants you didn't particularly like, get the travel agent involved, and let them use their leverage to get the action you desire.

Don't Lose Those Miles — Another post-trip tip is to pull together all of your boarding passes and ticket stubs and file them in your "frequent flyer" file so you can check your next quarterly mileage report against your records to ensure the airline has given you credit for all the miles you flew. If it appears that some of your trip legs were omitted, dig out as much evidence as you can about the flights you were on and send copies of the material to the airline involved. If you haven't kept good records of your flights, ask the travel agent to help you. Frequently, their computer printouts will give you the proof you need to get your report corrected.

Be A Pen Pal —Try to keep in touch with travelers you met during your trip. Exchange pictures and stories about your common experiences and try to maintain contact so you can compare notes the next time you plan a trip.

It's also a good idea to forward pictures that show your hosts enjoying your visit. A print of an appropriate picture is often a treasured gift for the host individual or family.

While you're at it, why not send a picture of yourself, showing you having a great time, to your travel agent? They'll get a lot of satisfaction from seeing you enjoying your trip experience.

Don't Be Shy — If you encountered a major problem during your trip, act quickly to resolve it upon your return. If a monetary loss has occurred, calculate that loss and report it to your agent. Unfortunately, there is no way to place a value on irritation, anxiety and disappointment, but compensation for tangible losses should be pursued.

Address a one-page typed letter to the person who handles consumer complaints or to the president or general manager of the company involved in the problem. Include travel dates, place where the problem occurred, and a specific description of the problem — identifying who was involved, if at all possible. Attach copies of your documentation and set a deadline for a response.

A few days after you mail the letter, follow up by phone to determine they received it and set a deadline date for action to be taken.

If the items in question were charged on a credit card, notify your bank or credit card company immediately that the matter is under review. Federal law enables you to dispute a charge within 60 days of the time it was posted on your bill. Write the credit card company or issuing bank and attach the statement and receipts.

Go For A Refund — If you haven't already done so, now's the time to apply for your Value-Added Tax refund. Gather up your receipts and send them to the customs authority of the countries visited. Be sure you pick up the necessary forms before you leave those countries.

Prepare For Next Trip — Inspect your luggage for damage or broken pieces. If your bags need to be replaced, be sure to select new bags on wheels, so you can maneuver more freely in airports.

Send Them Away — Knowing what to buy when it's gift-giving time is one of life's challenges that many busy people could easily live without. But one of today's best kept secrets could solve the problem nicely.

I'm referring to travel gift certificates, available from over 83 per cent of the nation's agents, according to the American Society of Travel Agents. Travel gifts can take the form of a transfer of frequent flyer miles or a nominal $25 cost for a certificate that is redeemable on hotel or meal charges.

Gift-givers with deeper pockets can choose from a variety of packages and certificate denominations. According to the *Chicago Tribune*, the high-end purchase might include a $43,500 "Around the World Tour" from Abercrombie & Kent International, Inc.

A more conventional purchase might be a weekend getaway certificate the recipient and his or her family would enjoy. A Marriott® hotel certificate, for example, could be redeemed at any Marriott® hotel in the company's network.

Another approach is to give up some of your frequent flyer miles as a gift. Major airlines allow customers to transfer their mileage awards to anyone for domestic flights, and give recipients up to a year to convert their award certificates to an actual ticket.

If you're constantly stumped about a gift choice, as I usually am, you might consider contacting your professional travel agent and exploring the options that gift certificates offer. Your appreciative recipient will enjoy redeeming their certificates and you won't have to worry whether the gift will fit or that the color will be compatible. What a deal.

22.

My Best To You

Live all you can; it's a mistake not to. It doesn't so much matter what you do in particular, so long as you have your life. If you haven't had that, what have you had?

— Henry James

The recollections I describe in this chapter represent my favorite venues for sightseeing, good food, and comfortable accommodations. You may differ with my choices, but I found these travel destinations to be extraordinary places to enjoy the finer aspects of travel.

City of the 21st Century

One of our planet's quietly emerging cities is Dresden, Germany, where Allied military intelligence (a well-documented oxymoron) went berserk near the end of World War II and destroyed in waves of fire-bomb raids — with questionable justification — 45,000 lives, countless buildings of classic architecture, and irreplaceable art treasures. Now five decades later, Dresden is still trying to recover from the sheer insanity of the military establishment, but the rebuilding process has succeeded to the point that the city's cultural center and graceful ambiance have been almost fully restored.

The new Dresden looks a lot like the Dresden of old. Like London, Rome and other European cities of note, this "Paris of the north" is built around a waterway — the Elbe River, which slices through the center of town. The riverfront facilitates the presence of dozens of pleasant cafes, restaurants, open air markets and coffee houses within the downtown area, all featuring clear views of the excursion and commercial boat traffic of the Elbe.

As a harsh reminder of the constantly present restoration process, a display outside of our downtown Hilton featured thousands of stone parts from a bombed-out Frauenkirche (Church of Our Lady) cathedral the city intends to rebuild when sufficient funding is available. Each part of the church, erected originally between 1726 and 1743, is carefully labeled to identify its position in the puzzle, and all of the remnant sections are housed on large steel shelves within plain view of all passers-by.

Tourists and residents alike are grateful that the renaissance of the city's cultural center is just about completed. Its philharmonic hall, baroque Semper Opera House, galleries, restaurants and hotels are jewels in this elegant re-creation of a cultured past. Dresden is an excellent example of how the efforts of intelligent people with high ideals can bring about a successful renewal that was necessitated by the ill-advised actions of a military establishment whose link with good sense and human compassion was nonexistent.

Nevertheless, Dresden is a city (population 480,000) to be explored and enjoyed for what it is today — a courageous survivor that came back stronger from its near-fatal condition to regain its standing as one of Europe's great cities.

And, if you're going to travel to Dresden, plan on a side trip to the luxurious Albrechtsberg Castle and to the Meissen Porcelain Manufactory, where some of the world's finest glazed porcelain pieces are handcrafted by meticulous artisans.

Finally, after you've scaled the mountain outside of Dresden in a cable car called the Schwebebahn, you'll realize that this is a city of peaks and valleys — and its current cycle is definitely in an up mode. See it soon.

Generations Have Looked Up to His Work

Any attempts I might make to describe the magnificent works of Michelangelo on the ceiling of the Sistine Chapel in the Vatican complex would be inadequate. The project, initiated in 1508 and finished in 1512, is regarded as one of the finest of his many incredible works. My wife Nancy and I visited the chapel after the latest restoration effort in 1994, so we had the opportunity to view the tones and hues of the ceiling as they appeared after its original completion.

The ceiling frescoes are divided into three zones, the highest showing scenes from Genesis. The Last Judgement over the altar was painted between 1535 and 1541. (Remember that there was no special temperature control while he worked and there were no hydraulic lifts to boost him into position each day).

The current director of the Vatican museums is considering limitations in the number of visitors allowed to enter the chapel. Three million people enjoy the magnificent frescoes annually.

Some 20 years or so after he finished the chapel ceiling, Michelangelo became the chief architect of St. Peter's Church, another monumental task. The massive, rock-solid edifice is the focal point of the Vatican and is symbolic of the strength of the Catholic faith.

During our stay in Rome, we participated in a Mass offici- ated by Pope John Paul II. The occasion was the celebration of an early stage of sainthood for an Italian holy man who died at a young age, and the special Mass was conducted outdoors in St. Peter's Square, with the basilica serving as a strikingly dramatic backdrop to the ceremony.

The congregation that day included 10,000 or more visi- tors like us, including the lady with the New York accent who showed up halfway through the service and asked, in a loud voice, "How do we get to see the pope?" At that very moment, he stood at the altar, not more than 50 yards from her location.

One of the amazing sights during the concluding phase of the Mass was the emergence of an army of priests through the doors of St. Peter's when it was time to serve communion to the throng of worshipers. As far as I could tell, every single person who wanted to participate received a host from one of the priest- helpers — many of whom were probably visitors as well.

From the scarlet and gold-garbed Swiss guards at the entry to St. Peter's Square to the Michelangelo works of art, the Vatican stands out as one of our most-enchanting all-time venues. If you're in Rome, do as visitors have for centuries and spend a few days touring the treasures of the Vatican for experiences you won't soon forget.

A Hotel That Forgot to Grow Up

Since Chicago is one of our favorite cities, we try to find reasons to go there often. One of our best motivations is the beautifully restored Whitehall Hotel, located in the heart of Chicago's upscale shopping district just off Michigan Avenue.

The Whitehall is a diminutive hotel by Chicago standards, with just 221 guest rooms and suites. But what it lacks in size is more than made up in service, one of its leading attributes.

From the moment we check in, we're looked after with care and warmth by the friendly staff. And when it's time to dine, the Whitehall Place offers an intimate setting with elegant selections, blended with the kind of service that makes other restaurants jealous.

During warmer months, you can dine alfresco on East Delaware Place in front of the hotel. Back inside, enjoy the musical artistry of local pianists starting at 5 p.m. Wednesdays through Saturdays. And the Whitehall Place Sunday brunch is a fabulous way to treat yourself to the finest buffet selection this side of Scandinavia.

Within a few short blocks of the Whitehall, we can visit the bustling Bloomingdale's®, Marshall Field's®, F.A.O. Schwarz®, Crate & Barrel®, and hundreds of other stores and boutiques that satisfy just about every imaginable need.

The Whitehall has been called "one of the eight great small hotels in the world" by *Fortune* magazine. In my opinion, they're both politically and judgmentally correct. I can't wait to visit the other seven.

A Bucket of Beer. Some Coffee Break!

There must be hundreds of "European-cuisine" ethnic restaurants in North America that promise "old world atmosphere," but there's only one that delivers the ambiance of a native German dining spot like Mader's in downtown Milwaukee. From the stunning "Jaeger Stübe" to the relatively new Knights Bar, this is the place to go for gemütlichkeit (warm hospitality) and the best of German cuisine.

When it was known as "The Comfort," before 1919, it was said to be the era of the "bucket boys" who carried a board with hooks from which a half dozen pails of cool, frothy beer hung

while the boys made the rounds of the downtown office buildings. Their eagerly-awaited refreshment was passed around to all of the workers, making the absence of air conditioning almost bearable.

Mader's survived Prohibition, the Great Depression, and World War II. During the war years, the Mader family de-emphasized the German theme for obvious reasons, but resumed offering standard fare after the war, including sauerbraten, wiener schnitzel and pork shank — menu favorites that have been retained to this day.

In a city known for its penchant for German food, Mader's offers an unequaled dining experience that keeps discriminating aficionados of fine food coming back for more.

Except for the bucket brigade, it presents its extensive menu of choices in the same mode as it did in the '30s and '40s, with much the same atmosphere that exists in the fine old building of today. C'mon — visit Mader's someday soon. You won't be disappointed; and you won't have to drink their many beer selections out of buckets.

23.

Look To The Future

*For I dipt into the future, far as human
eye could see,
Saw the vision of the world, and all the
wonder that would be.*

— Alfred, Lord Tennyson

Individual movie screens, personal video games, air-to-ground faxes, and other electronic communications innovations are only the start of a revolution in air travel. In first class cabins of some of its jumbo jets, Japan Airlines is testing a new Sky Massage seat, which works over the tired traveler's body. Customers can even pick the type of 15-minute rub they'd like: shiatsu (pressure), rolling, or pounding.

Looking ahead to air travel beyond the year 2000, the computer will play an even more critical role than today. A speaker at a recent conference sponsored by NASA predicted that computers — not pilots — will operate the planes of the future. Using satellites as guiding devices, planes will be routed via computer technology to their destination without the presence of a pilot

— and all eventualities enroute will be addressed by the preprogrammed computer "brain".

While computers may pilot the aircraft of the future, they're already popular companions for many air travelers in the passenger cabin. But the batteries can run down during a long flight, leaving the laptops useless.

Delta Airlines to the rescue. Delta offers inflight power sources for laptops on some of its Boeing 767 jets, providing the contact right at the seat for computer operation or convenient battery recharging. Other airlines are likely to offer the same service in the near future.

There are undoubtedly many other amenities coming in the aircraft of the future. Here are some I'd like to include on my shopping list:

◆ Bathrooms that are a bit larger than phone booths;

◆ Computer equipment that can be ordered in advance like special meals;

◆ A menu of movies you can choose from for your private TV monitor;

◆ Travel films covering the country or region you're heading for;

◆ Educational programs you can select between meal servings;

◆ A lounge where you can stand up and stretch while on long overseas flights.

What would you include on your list?

*   *   *

In the travel agent business, you can look for a number of significant trends that will influence the way you travel. One that you can count on is growth in the number of agencies that take on affiliations with national membership organizations that maintain high standards of performance and provide huge buying power, resulting in better values for their customers.

The trend, which is already underway, will parallel movement in the real estate business toward national organizations like Century 21®.

Hickory Travel Systems, for example, enables independent agents to continue in business "for themselves, but not by themselves." As a result, the local relationship between the customer and agent is maintained, but the agency can capitalize on the benefits of national affiliations — bringing the traveler top hotel discounts, the best deals with travel suppliers, and other savings that "clout" in the marketplace can bring.

One of the chief advantages of a nationwide organization like Hickory is their ability to "wheel and deal" with hotels to set aside large blocks of rooms at guaranteed preferred rates. Often, that translates to the availability of rooms when the entire city may be sold out due to convention business. Also, the hotels provide extra-value amenities with these rooms, including upgrades, complimentary breakfasts, in-room movies, newspapers, access to health clubs, and others.

It's a good idea to ask your travel agent whether they have national affiliations with a major network. If they do, you can be confident that you'll be getting the best travel bargains by dealing with them. When you work with a Hickory Travel Systems agent, you'll enjoy extra value features like emergency service, 24-hour reservation system, car discount programs, and expert round the world support.

24.

About
That Lunch. . .

Weary with toil, I haste me to my bed
The dear repose for limbs with travel tired:
But then begins a journey in my head
To work my mind, when body's work's expired.
— William Shakespeare

Taking your travel agent to lunch can be one of the best moves a traveler can make to:

a. Learn what's new in the travel game;

b. Develop a rapport with someone who knows how to minimize your cost and maximize your value for flights and hotels;

c. Find out that your frequent flyer coupons expired last week.

The whole idea of lunching with a travel agent is my way of recommending that a friendly, lasting relationship with a knowledgeable travel agent can pay dividends repeatedly whenever you decide to travel by plane, train, or cruise ship.

Once the agent gets to know you, understands your travel

needs and preferences, and becomes aware of your travel and lifestyle goals, he or she will be able to do a much more effective job of planning future trip packages than if you show up as a last minute, one time, price-only shopper.

Most travel agents realize that their survival over the long haul depends upon their ability to find, satisfy and retain clients for many years and for many trips. Therefore, they are as anxious as you are to make the relationship work to your benefit.

In my extensive travels over the past 35-plus years, I've never encountered a travel agent who was out for the "fast buck" — to pad the profit on a trip package at my expense. The people I have worked with have always treated me with respect, with honesty, and with a sincere interest in helping me get the most pleasure possible out of my travel investment.

As Bill Chiles points out, there's no need to take a chance and risk a bad travel experience by buying travel sight unseen.

"A travel agent," he advises, "is able to recognize loss leaders for what they are as well as identify unreliable carriers, uncomfortable or unsafe hotels, and marginal cruise lines. Otherwise, it's like someone trying to do someone else's job without training or experience. The likelihood is that you will make the wrong assumptions and arrive at the wrong decisions in your travel arrangements because of your lack of experience."

There's no logical reason why you can't enjoy success in travel planning. But you must be committed to making an effort to find the agent best qualified to fulfill your needs and demands. As with most things in life, doing your homework upfront will generally result in "Class A" results when you finally take that trip for which you have been waiting a long time.

If you're as fortunate as I have been to enjoy many travel opportunities during your lifetime, make the most of each of them. I have few regrets about past travels, but one of them is that I could have done a better job of preparing for each trip. Greater knowledge of the history and traditions behind each destination would have provided a useful framework for my experiences and made them more meaningful. This kind of information is readily available from your travel agent.

I wish that I had maintained contact with people I met overseas during my travels. One of the outstanding benefits of the Internet is, I believe, the opportunity for low-cost, convenient communications with people all over the globe. For example, I have been able to maintain ongoing dialogue monthly with Werner Richter, a university professor whom I visited during a trip last year to Capetown, South Africa, by e-mailing messages to him.

Keeping in touch with people you've met in distant lands is one of life's enriching experiences, and I encourage you to communicate regularly with those you meet overseas on future trips after you return home. It's part of the "broadening" aspect of quality travel, and the relationships you develop often outlast local friendships.

My final regret is that I didn't expose our three sons to more travel experiences prior to their departure from the "nest." Sure, we did the Disney thing and took them on occasional business trips. But I'm talking about heavy-duty travel throughout North America and in foreign lands.

Ulrich Liedtke, a European friend of mine, bought round-the-world flight tickets for each of his two sons and sent them on their way with minimal financial support. Both returned home months later with in-depth knowledge of the distinctions in world cultures and travel memories they will treasure for a lifetime.

Take a travel agent to lunch? Why not? You may even get them to buy (fat chance!). Do it soon, and enjoy their professional services for a long time to come.

If You Wait, It May Be Too Late

When you're on some foreign shore
And exciting experiences come your way
Enjoy them all and search for more
For life may never be as beautiful
as it is today.

As the Eiffel Tower and Big Ben beckon
And you do as the Romans do in Rome
Cruise on the Thames and then, you'll reckon,
That it's time for your special touch of home.

Whether you're from NY or West L.A.
It's always fun to get up and get away.
But when it's over you'll sit back down
And savor trip memories for many a day.

Travel adventures arrive and then depart
And new experiences come your way
Enjoy them all and search for more
For life may never be as beautiful
as it is today.

– Harry Knitter

APPENDIX I

Frequent Flyer Programs

Your travel agent will keep a record of your frequent flyer club membership and ensure that your code number is entered on each ticket and boarding pass so you get all of the miles you have earned. Also, they will provide a record of your trips throughout the year, so you can check the rundown against your statements from the airlines. To enroll in frequent flyer programs or obtain information about your mileage account, keep this list handy:

American Airlines	Advantage Desk	(800) 882-8880
America West	Flight Fund Desk	(800) 247-5691
Continental Airlines	One Pass	(713) 952-1630
Delta Air Lines	Frequent Flyer	(800) 323-2323
Midwest Express	Frequent Flyer	(800) 452-2022
Northwest Airlines	WorldPerks	(800) 447-3757
TWA	F.F. Bonus	(800) 325-4815
United Air Lines	Mileage-Plus	(605) 399-2400
USAir Freq. Traveler	Service Center	(800) 872-4738

APPENDIX II

Who To Contact To Resolve Problems

If you have a complaint about a travel agent or would like to check out their certification qualifications, it's a good idea to contact the appropriate association or governmental agency that can provide the information you need. Here are the leading associations and agencies for your reference:

American Society of Travel Agents
Consumer Affairs
1101 King Street
Alexandria, VA 22314
(703) 739-2782

Institute of Certified Travel Agents
148 Linden Street
Wellesley, MA 02181
(701) 237-0280

Association of Retail Travel Agents
845 Sir Thomas Court, Suite 3
Harrisburg, PA 17109
(717) 545-9548

Here are some additional points of contact that you may find helpful:

U.S. Tour Operators Association
211 E. 51st Street, Suite 12B
New York, NY 10022

The Department of Transportation
Consumer Affairs Office
  400 Seventh Street, S.W.
  Washington, D.C. 20590
  (202) 366-2220

Cruise Ship Complaints:

The Federal Maritime Commission
  Office of Informal Inquiries and Complaints
  800 N. Capitol Street, N.W.
  Washington, D.C. 20573

U.S. Coast Guard
  Foreign Passenger Vessel Program
  2100 Second Street, S.W.
  Washington D.C. 20593

INDEX

About the Collaborator
L. William Chiles

As one of the travel industry's most successful and innovative executives, L. William Chiles knows the business as well as a cruise ship captain knows the waters his vessel will sail. He has extensive experience in both corporate and incentive sectors and serves on the advisory boards of both the Airline Reporting Corporation (ARC) and the American Society of Travel Agents (ASTA), as well as other industry and tourism organizations. Globally, he serves as deputy chairman of the board of directors of First Business Travel International.

In 1989, he was appointed president and chief executive officer of Hickory Travel Systems, Inc. Under his leadership, the company has grown to become the industry's first "supernetwork" of 1,500 member locations, a $7 billion-plus worldwide travel organization. Its world class hotel discount program, 24-hour reservations center, international rate desk, training, automation, marketing and other benchmark programs are setting the standards for the industry.

Chiles' travel industry experience includes senior management positions as vice-president of sales and marketing for Carlson Companies' travel group and incentive/marketing divisions.

He brings to the travel industry a rich and varied background. He served as president and CEO of Cory Corporation, the office services and convenience stores subsidiary of Hershey Foods Corporation, and as president and CEO of EMRA Corporation (dba Supercuts).

Chiles holds degrees in marketing and finance from Colorado State University.

About the Author
Harry Knitter

Harry Knitter has always loved writing, having discovered the magic of written communications when, as a young boy, he air-mailed notes to his four uncles who were stationed overseas during World War II. In return, they sent him souvenir military cloth shoulder patches, and each time he received a parcel from Europe he was motivated to write a response letter reporting tidbits of family news.

Later, while in college in Wisconsin, he decided that his passion for writing would be transformed into the focal point of his career. He subsequently wrote for several newspapers and developed sales presentations, created commercials, wrote press releases, and produced copy for brochures and a wide range of print advertising and promotion communications for The West Bend Company, Chrysler, Ross Roy Advertising, FTD and the John Henry Company, his employers.

At the present time, he is the vice-president of creative marketing services for The John Henry Company of Lansing, Michigan, a major supplier to the retail florist, horticultural, and pharmaceutical industries.

After a successful 36-year career in marketing, during which he traveled extensively, Harry started writing nonfiction pieces for publication in 1995. His first book, *Holding Pattern: Airport Waiting Made Easy*, has received worldwide media coverage and is delighting travelers all over North America.

ORDER INFORMATION

Send $9.95 plus $3.50 for shipping and handling for a copy of:

Holding Pattern: Airport Waiting Made Easy
by Harry Knitter

Holding Pattern helps you:
❖ Reduce travel stress and anxiety
❖ Enjoy stimulating ways to use idle time
❖ Relive the author's most interesting travel experiences
❖ Find out his favorite city, sights, hotels, and restaurants
❖ Prepare for future travel

To order, call 1-888-567-3363 or
1-888-KORDENE
Send your check or money order to:
KORDENE PUBLICATIONS
4463 Copperhill Drive
Okemos, MI 48864

Michigan Residents ADD 60¢ Per Book For State Sales Tax